First published in 2012 by Millgate House Publishers.

Millgate House Publishers is an imprint of
Millgate House Education Ltd
Unit 1, Zan Business Park,
Crewe Road,
Sandbach,
Cheshire,
CW11 4QD
UK

Edited by Brenda Keogh and Stuart Naylor.

Graphics, layout and CD ROM design by Millgate House Education Ltd.

Printed by Cambrian Printers.

British Library Cataloguing in Publication Data
A catalogue record for this book is available from the British Library.

ISBN 978-0-9562646-1-9

Acknowledgements

Writing a book can be a solitary occupation. Those people who provide advice, support and guidance are invaluable to any author.

With that in mind I would like to thank the following individuals most sincerely for their insightful comments, unending patience and uplifting humour:

- The Heads and teachers at Llangorse Church in Wales Primary School, Talgarth Primary School and Bronllys Primary School, who generously set time aside for the children to take part in the 'Look, Think, Talk' activities. It is the photographs of the delightful children in the schools that bring these activities to life.

- All of the Millgate House Education team, especially Brenda Keogh, Jo Williams, Neil Pepper and Stuart Naylor, for reviewing, carefully editing the book and so skillfully managing the publishing process.

- And finally, my husband, Peter, who provides unfailing encouragement and endless cups of weak tea while I'm tip-tapping away on my laptop!

Index

The text in brackets indicates the key concepts, skills and types of enquiry that can be developed through the activities. A range of additional concepts, skills and types of enquiry is identified within the activity chapters.

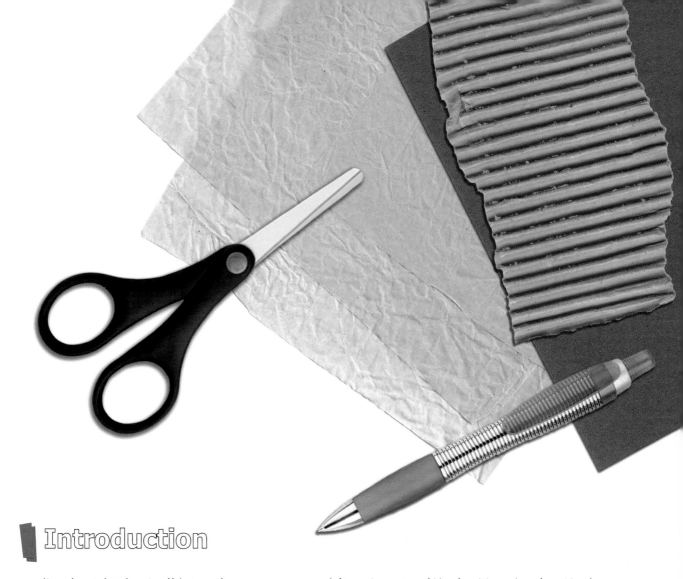

Introduction

'Look, Think, Talk' is the partner publication to *'Made You Look, Made You Think, Made You Talk'*. *'Look, Think, Talk'* is aimed at 7-12 year olds. *'Made You Look'* is aimed 3-8 year olds. Both books provide a series of simple, stimulating starting point activities that encourage children to **look**, **think** and **talk** about what they experience. In addition they describe a range of strategies that support the activities, challenge children's ideas and develop good knowledge, understanding and skills. There are also opportunities for children to communicate their experiences effectively. In this way, the activities become more than simply good fun.

'Look, Think, Talk' follows the same format as *'Made You Look'*, although a number of additions appropriate to older children have been made. The format of the book is described in detail on the next page.

All activities have a clear purpose and conceptual focus, and encourage children to strive to solve problems; they are not designed to be mere demonstrations done by the teacher. Everyday materials and resources are suggested throughout.

Each activity in *'Look, Think, Talk'* contains extension ideas to enhance the activity and to develop children's understanding. The strategies underpinning these extension ideas are described on pages 11 to 27.

Each chapter includes:

• Guidelines for how to prepare and use the activity

This section includes key concepts, details of resources, guidance for using the activity and key questions that you might ask. It also identifies potential health and safety issues. We recommend ASE's *Be safe!* (2011) for working safely with children when carrying out science activities.

• Ideas for extension activities and cross-curricular links

The activities in this section use Active Assessment strategies, to challenge children's ideas and take their thinking further. They make thinking, learning and assessment an active and engaging process for children. The way that these strategies are used can also lead children into wanting to learn more about something, so that assessment and learning become integrated into one seamless process.

For each activity, one of the suggested strategies is developed in some detail to show how it can be used. A worksheet is provided to support the activity. Worksheets and other resources are available **on the CD** so that they can be printed out.

In addition, each chapter contains ideas for making cross-curricular links. The suggested links enable children to apply skills and concepts gained through the science activities, and reinforce and extend their learning. In this way, you can make the best use of curriculum time and children see a purpose and value to their learning.

● Looking for evidence of thinking and learning

Engaging the children in exploring science in a happy, supported lesson, and allowing time and space to think and discuss their understanding, will provide many opportunities to recognise, assess and celebrate progress. To help you in this process, the section contains suggestions for the concepts and skills children might learn and experience through the activities. The following section outlines the main activities where children can develop their ideas and understanding. The final section identifies the nature of the evidence of their thinking and learning. It shows that there are many contexts in which thinking and learning can be observed. Children do not need to demonstrate all of these to be successful.

Looking for evidence of thinking and learning

In this activity children have the opportunity to:
- ✓ develop their observational skills
- ✓ develop their skills of comparing physical features of animals such as eyes, structures for breathing, sensing, eating, communicating, etc.
- ✓ develop their understanding of classifying and grouping
- ✓ use and explore the meaning of scientific vocabulary such as skull, antennae, mouth parts, bone, chitin, etc.
- ✓ learn about adaptation to the environment in animals
- ✓ develop their skills of sorting information onto tables and graphic organisers

They can do this by:
- ✓ observing a range of photographs of animal heads
- ✓ using Compare and contrast graphic organisers and Carroll diagrams
- ✓ identifying particular physical adaptations in animals
- ✓ responding to Most likely to questions
- ✓ taking part in a Splat! game
- ✓ analysing photographs and maps

You should see evidence of their thinking and learning in:
- ✓ What they say to you and each other about their observations
- ✓ the Compare and contrast graphic organisers and Carroll diagrams that they produce
- ✓ their explanations about adaptation as they view the photographs
- ✓ how they discuss and answer Most likely to questions
- ✓ how they engage in the Splat! activity
- ✓ their comments while analysing photographs and maps

HEADS 12

99

© Gaynor Weavers 2012

The 'Looking for evidence of thinking and learning' section is based on a framework developed by Brenda Keogh and Stuart Naylor, first published in Bird and Saunders (2007).

• What children do

Photographs of what the children might do or write are included here. This includes drawings, diagrams, written work and models.

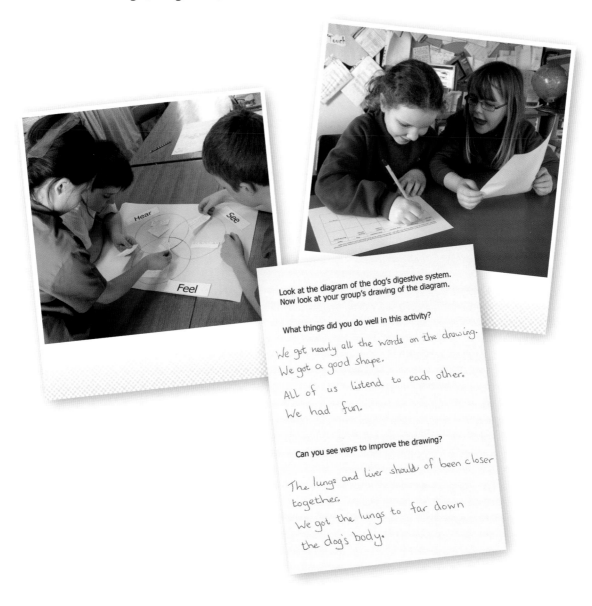

Look at the diagram of the dog's digestive system.
Now look at your group's drawing of the diagram.

What things did you do well in this activity?

We got nearly all the words on the drawing.
We got a good shape.
ALL of us listend to each other.
We had fun.

Can you see ways to improve the drawing?

The lungs and liver should of been closer together.
We got the lungs to far down the dog's body.

• Reviewing the learning

This section provides questions that you could use to help children to review the activities and their own learning. The questions also help children to explore how they develop their understanding and the strategies they use for learning and problem solving (metacognition). At the end of an activity, or at any other appropriate point, children can also be asked, *'What made you think that?'* or *'What made you change your mind?'*

Strategies used as starting points for the extension activities

This section explains and exemplifies the strategies used in 'Look, Think, Talk' to support an Active Assessment approach to extending children's learning. The strategies are drawn from a range of ideas and sources including those of the author, Gaynor Weavers, as well as from Active Assessment (Naylor, Keogh and Goldsworthy (2004) and DCELLS (2006), 'The Thinking Skills and Assessment for Learning Programme', Qualifications, Curriculum & Assessment Authority for Wales, 2006, 'Curriculum Planning for Primary Schools: Science', M. Tibbott & G. Weavers, (ESIS) 1998, 'Progress in Learning: Science', M. Tibbott & G. Weavers (ESIS & CCBC), 2006 together with other curriculum development work of the author.

The strategies offer a way to build on children's interest and extend and consolidate their learning. They are designed to create opportunities for children to observe, think, discuss and explore their ideas. The **accompanying CD contains worksheets** for each extension activity, some of which include deliberate mistakes to provide additional challenge for children.

Many of these strategies can be used by individuals. If used in this way at the end of a topic or science enquiry, they can be a valuable summative assessment tool. However, when used as starting points or extension activities, they have a greater impact on learning where children are encouraged to talk with each other and work collaboratively. In this way, children challenge each other's ideas and make explicit what they do and do not think and know. This combination of self and peer assessment helps children to become active in the learning process. Used in this way they are valuable formative assessment tools. Younger or less confident children may need some support or teacher mediation.

Crucially, it is what is done with the outcomes of the strategies that makes them effective for formative assessment of children's understanding. For example, at the end of the lesson it is helpful to get children to review changes in their ideas and how the strategies have helped them to learn. Examples of questions to help children to review their learning are included at the end of each activity.

In the information that follows, if the strategy is used as the main strategy to extend an activity, 'MS' appears in brackets after the Activity number. There is more detail about them in each section of the book and a children's Worksheet is provided on the CD incorporating the suggested strategy.

Annotated Drawing

We often ask children to draw their observations or to express their ideas pictorially, but asking them to include words or annotate their drawing allows them to add more detail to what they see or think. For example, some children may not be skilled enough to show a dimpled orange skin, but can use a word or two to express what the skin looks or feels like. Words can be scribed when extra support is needed.

In some cases, it is valuable to ask for annotated drawings at both the beginning and at the end of a topic. When children see for themselves how much they have learned, it can inspire them to observe more carefully in future. An example of Annotated Drawing can be found in Activity 8, Milk Explosion.

Card Sort

In this activity, children work with a partner to consider a set of statements on small cards. They must decide whether they agree or disagree with each statement and sort the cards into columns headed 'Agree', 'Disagree' or 'It depends!'

Wherever they choose to put the cards, children need to know that they must be able to explain their thinking to you or another pair of classmates. An example of a Card Sort can be found in Activity 19 (MS), Celebration Candles.

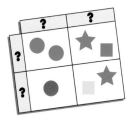

Carroll Diagrams

A Carroll Diagram, seen widely in primary classrooms, is a simple diagram used for grouping items or objects. The most common type is a grid that sorts by two properties - either having a particular attribute or not having that attribute. For example, animals may be sorted by 'wings' or 'not wings' and '6 legs' or 'not 6 legs'.

These diagrams allow children to explore their ideas about objects according to their properties and then work together to present this information. An example of a Carroll Diagram can be found in Activity 12, Heads.

Classifying and Grouping

Classifying and Grouping activities provide opportunities for children to discuss different possibilities, explain their ideas to each other and then try to reach consensus. They learn how to observe carefully, look for patterns and make generalisations. While they are doing this, they can provide evidence of their developing understanding.

We tend to use Classifying and Grouping interchangeably, though they are subtly different. When we classify, we usually use given criteria to sort things; when we group, we usually put things into groups where the criteria are not fixed in advance. An example of Classifying and Grouping can be found in Activity 6, Marble Drop.

Compare and Contrast Graphic Organiser

Compare and Contrast is a very useful approach for enabling children to develop their observational skills. The strategy is most often used when the items under scrutiny have areas of similarity and difference. For example a spider and a housefly could be compared in terms of how they move, how many legs they have, what shape their bodies are and so on.

Graphic Organisers provide additional support for thinking and learning as children try to reach agreement about their ideas, as well as direct evidence of their understanding. An example of a Compare and Contrast Graphic Organiser can be found in Activity 12 (MS), Heads, Activity 17 (MS), Shaky Changes, and in Activity 7, Sharing Memory.

Concept Cartoons®

Concept Cartoons (Naylor & Keogh, 2010) are cartoon-style drawings showing different characters arguing about an everyday situation. They are designed to intrigue, provoke discussion and stimulate scientific thinking.

The text is minimal and in dialogue form with alternative viewpoints on the situation. The scientifically acceptable viewpoint is included in the alternatives. An example of a Concept Cartoon can be found in Activity 16, Sound Circus (Drums) and in Activity 19, Celebration Candles (The Snowman's Coat).

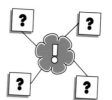

Concept Map

A good way to organise information is to construct a Concept Map (Novak & Gowin, 1984). These can stimulate ideas and help children think creatively. Working together to construct a Concept Map helps children to explore their ideas about a subject and identify new information they need to learn.

The individual words, drawings or concepts are shown in bubbles or boxes. Lines are drawn to link the concepts and words are written on these lines. Arrowheads show which way to read the links. Words can be generated by the children or you to give a range of ideas to discuss. On those occasions where the children do not have sufficient writing skills, you can take on the role of scribe.

By noting the links that children are making within the Concept Map, you can identify which areas are well understood and which are causing a problem. If used at the start and then the end of a topic, it is possible to see how much learning has taken place. Displaying the two Concept Maps impresses children with how much more they have learned too. An example of a Concept Map can be found in Activity 10 (MS), Mix It Up!

Concept Sentences

In the Concept Sentence strategy (Naylor, Keogh & Goldsworthy, 2004), children are given a set of small cards, each of which contains a word relevant to the topic under study. These key words are moved about to create sentences. The activity helps children to explore their understanding of particular concepts using scientific vocabulary and can lead to further investigations.

You should select any key words carefully, including a selection of nouns, adjectives and verbs. You can include connectives to make sentence construction easier for less confident learners, but this can restrict the choice of words more confident learners use. A few blank cards should be included so that children can add their own words. An example of Concept Sentences can be found in Activity 3 (MS), Slow Melt.

Create a Story

Stories are exciting, enjoyable and fun. Setting a problem or series of facts in a story format can make it more real and help to engage children more quickly. If children work together to create their own stories they will be challenged to share their ideas, consider new possibilities, describe what is happening, explain their thinking and research and develop new ideas. An example of Create a Story can be found in Activity 10, Mix It Up!

Deliberate Mistakes

As the name suggests, this strategy relies on you showing or doing something which is incorrect, and the children spotting what's happened. This strategy helps children clarify their own ideas by observation and discussion with others and to identify what else they may need to do or learn in order to correct the mistakes.

Alternatively, you can ask children to deliberately generate mistakes themselves. They can add some mistakes to information that they have researched and then swap notes with others to see how quickly their deliberate mistakes can be found.

This sort of strategy works well as a small group exercise. It is useful for assessing how learners respond to the deliberate mistakes. For example, do they notice them and how do they think they should be corrected? An example of Deliberate Mistakes can be found in Activity 20, Comparative Circus.

Expert Witness

Children are challenged to work together to become 'experts' on different concepts or aspects of a topic by carrying out independent research. After a period of study, classmates raise appropriate questions for the experts to answer in a limited time. Any questions that cannot be answered can be recorded for further research.

The strategy encourages children to work independently to identify what they already understand and what else they need to learn and to have control of the information to be relayed to their classmates. An example of Expert Witness can be found in Activity 4, Eat Your Words.

50:50

Children are better able to understand and recall information if they have talked about it or taught it to others. During 50:50 children work in pairs, although trios or even fours also work well. Each child has some of the information needed to finish a task or challenge, such as making an informative poster for younger children. The children look at what they have been given and then join another class member to share their information. They also need to make sure that what they communicate is easily understood.

50:50 allows children to work with others and share data or information — a skill that supports many areas of the curriculum. An example of 50:50 can be found in Activity 16, Sound Circus.

Goldfish Bowl

In this case a whole group discusses the topic they have been studying and another group watches and listens carefully. They then reverse roles so that the second group can discuss the first group's and their own ideas. Finally both groups work together to identify things where they agree and don't agree and ideas that need clarifying, leading to new research and learning. An example of Goldfish Bowl can be found in Activity 15, Ballooning.

Jigsawing

The Jigsawing strategy offers a structure for group work, promotes speaking and listening, and encourages the sharing of ideas and further research.

The class forms small Home Groups. Each child is delegated a question or aspect of a topic to research and become the 'expert' on that area. If they are looking at butterflies, for example, they might study where the insects live, what they eat, how they differ in appearance or the stages in their life cycle. Children researching the same feature work together before returning to their Home Groups to share what they have found out. An example of Jigsawing can be found in Activity 5 (MS), Veg Tops and in Activity 2, Colourful Caterpillars.

Just a Minute

Here pairs, or groups, of children work together to research a topic such as caterpillars. An identification guide is given to each child at the beginning and they focus on one caterpillar in particular. Children take turns to talk about their caterpillar for a whole minute. Classmates can question them for further information, which helps to identify any ideas that need to be developed further.

As an alternative, run this game as a class activity with two teams or as a small group activity with individual opponents. If anything is said that is incorrect, they can be challenged and the opposing team can take over.

This strategy encourages individual and group collaboration and research. Children need to think up incisive questions and be able to respond fluently to an audience. An example of Just a Minute can be found in Activity 2, Colourful Caterpillars, Activity 5, Veg Tops, and in Activity 15, Ballooning.

KWHL Grid

These simple 4-column grids set out what learners **K**now about a topic, what they **W**ant to know about it, **H**ow they will find out and then what they have **L**earnt by the end. In principle, these grids can be used by individual children but as an Active Assessment strategy children working together on a grid is more productive.

- You, or groups of children, discuss a topic, such as plant reproduction, to find out what they think they know
- any points that they make can be recorded in the first column
- then the children can decide what they would like to know for the second column
- next they need to decide how to find out this information
- finally, after their research or enquiries, the last column can be completed to show what they have found out.

The main strength of this process is that it starts from children's ideas. Misconceptions and previous learning can be identified and children are actively involved in their own learning. If you are beginning a unit of work, the KWHL Grid helps identify gaps in knowledge. At the end, it allows children to reflect on their understanding and learning. This can then be applied to new situations. An example of a KWHL Grid can be found in Activity 4 (MS), Eat Your Words.

Listening Trios

Children work in groups of three and take the role of the Talker, the Questioner or the Recorder.

- The Talker chooses an item, for example, a body part, tells the other two and then begins to describe that body part clearly, explaining its job in the body and how useful it is to our lives.
- The Questioner must listen carefully, prompt the talker into further description and ask for any clarification when necessary.
- The Recorder listens and makes notes of the conversation. This report is read out at the end of the conversation.

When the activity is over, all three children discuss whether anything needs to be added to the report before the class meets for the final feedback session. Children can then swap roles and select another body part, or they can read the results of other Trios and discuss the outcomes. Results of the Listening Trios can be displayed with annotated posters. The names of the items can also be written on cards for the children to choose from. An example of Listening Trios can be found in Activity 1 (MS), Stick and Think.

Living Graph

In a Living Graph, children study a bar chart or line graph and interpret or justify the position of statements on the graph. The data given shows events or changes over time. Ambiguous statements may be included. Children position the set of related statements on the graph and must explain their ideas clearly.

For younger children, display a graph with labelled axes and ask them to describe what the graph shows. Challenge them to work together to predict the future path of a simple line graph showing, for example, plant growth.

With older children, or those more confident in using graphs, pairs or groups can be presented with some statements on paper labels to 'annotate' the given graph. These statements describe what may have 'happened' during the enquiry. Following discussion, each label is placed on the graph. This will provoke further debate and may lead to statements being moved to different areas. This continues until the group comes to a consensus. Once agreement is reached, the labels can be attached to the graph to produce a final record. An example of a Living Graph can be found in Activity 14 (MS), Blossoms.

Loop Cards

Children are each given a card. The cards contain a word on one half and the definition of a different word on the other half. Children read out the definition from their own card. All the other children look to see if they've got the word that matches that definition. The child who thinks they have the best match reads the word, and if all agree, then reads the definition from his or her card and so on. As an Active Assessment strategy it is helpful for children to work in pairs or play the loop card game within a group. An example of Loop Cards can be found in Activity 10, Mix it Up!

Making a List

This is a simple method for children to share ideas and share their knowledge or ideas about, for example, objects, events, plants or animals. It is a useful start to a topic when you want children to explore their current knowledge and understanding or generate ideas for an enquiry.

Depending on the children's age and ability, Making a List can be done by individuals, small groups or the whole class, and you may need to collate any words or ideas raised. However, if individuals provide lists, they will be evidence of each child's ideas. Whereas, when used as part of a group activity, the activity will be a stimulus to discussion and further learning. An example of Making a List can be found in Activity 7, Sharing Memory.

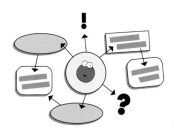

Mind Map®

Mind Maps, created by Tony Buzan in the 1970s (*Buzan, 1974*), help to structure information in a simple, visual way, using patterns, colours, pictures and associations. They are used to help analyse, understand and recall ideas and concepts. Most Mind Maps are drawn in landscape format.

A word or picture is put at the centre of the page.

- Related words or pictures are placed around the central image and connected to it with lines.

- Each of these related words can generate subtopics themselves, which can be joined to them with further lines.

- It is recommended that children use colour, drawings and symbols in the creation of Mind Maps to make them as visually attractive as possible.

- Varying text size, colour and alignment also helps, as does experimenting with the thickness and length as well as the colour of the lines.

Working together on Mind Maps helps children to explore, organise and challenge each other's ideas. It can also help to identify areas that need clarifying and where new learning is needed. Children can return to their Mind Maps and add new ideas. Children can be impressed by how much they have learned. An example of a Mind Map can be found in Activity 4, Eat Your Words.

Most Likely To

In this strategy children work in groups. They can be shown photographs, video or music. These are referred to as the children answer your questions and justify their decisions or predictions.

For example, you could give each group a set of photographs of foods. Ask them to answer questions such as, 'Where would you be most likely to see this food growing?', 'Which people are most likely to eat this food?' 'What makes you say that?'

The strategy encourages the children to think carefully about their own and other children's answers as every speculation has to be supported by evidence or a reasonable prediction. It may also lead to further research if there is uncertainty. An example of Most Likely To can be found in Activity 12, Heads.

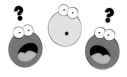

News Report

Asking the children to explore their knowledge and understanding by analysing a real or imaginary news report enhances their engagement with the topic and encourages them to think about science in everyday life. It is particularly useful where children need to think carefully about the pros and cons of a debate — for example, where they need to research the content of the report and challenge the views of one or more of the contributors.

Provide small groups or pairs with a real or mock page from a newspaper or a sheet of quotes about a current topic from a TV or radio interview. Give them time to look critically at and then discuss the science contained within the report. Do they agree with all of the points given? Is there an area where the science is incorrect or inaccurate? Adding questions about the News Report allows the children to think carefully about their own understanding before they answer. Once the children are familiar and comfortable with this strategy, they can use their knowledge and their creativity to compose their own News Reports. An example of a News Report can be found in Activity 2 (MS), Colourful Caterpillars.

Odd One Out

This strategy helps children to develop an understanding of key concepts and of vocabulary. It develops the understanding of classification in science. It also helps learners to understand the properties of different things. A list or set of pictures are shown and the question asked, 'Which is the odd one out?' If there is more than one possible answer this can lead to mature class discussion and helps develop the higher order skill of explanation. For example, "Duck, Seagull, Frog, Sparrow. Think about - Where they live; how they move; their legs; and so on. Which is the odd one out?" An example of Odd One Out can be found in Activity 6 (MS), Marble Drop and in Activity 17, Shaky Changes.

Posters

Asking children to create large Posters related to a topic allows them to work together to explore their ideas, research facts or data, and represent them so that essential information is displayed. The work can also be attached to a task or challenge and, in this case, the children can illustrate their thinking about the problem. An example of Posters can be found in Activity 3, Slow Melt.

Post-it Challenge

Children can work in small groups. Within a time limit they jot on Post-its three things they know about a specified object, for example an organ or part of the body, such as the heart. Call groups forward to the board to stick their Post-its around the targeted word - 'heart'. You might want to group the responses into those about its position, structure, function, importance to the body and so on. Read each note aloud and see if the class agrees. Encourage them to do more thinking and research where there is disagreement or uncertainty. Subsequently, children can research and compare the object to something else, for example parts of other animals. An example of Post-it Challenge can be found in Activity 1, Stick and Think.

Predict, Observe, Explore, Explain

In this strategy you ask the children to follow the sequence of:
  - **p**redicting what they think will happen next
  - **o**bserving what actually happens
  - **e**xploring what has happened
  - trying to **e**xplain what has happened.

(See White and Gunstone, 1992).

You can use POEE to probe children's understanding of what they are seeing. POEE is best used after children have made careful observations of what is happening, for example, when food colour and washing up liquid are added to milk. An example of POEE can be found in Activity 8 (MS), Milk Explosion and in Activity 13 (MS), Can Can.

Question Swap

Ask the children to research and prepare a set of cards each one containing a question and its answer on a chosen topic, for example the Water Cycle. Each child in the class needs a card. It helps if there are a few spares too. Each child then finds a partner.

The first child asks a question. If the partner does not know the answer, the first child can tell them. Clues can be given if agreed beforehand. Then the second child asks his or her question. Once both questions are asked and answered, the children can swap cards. Then they put up their hand to show they are ready for another partner. Ask them to identify any questions where they don't agree on the answer. These can be shared with the whole class and researched further to try to reach agreement. An example of Question Swap can be found in Activity 11, Water Cycle Seedlings.

Sentence Cards

This is a fun approach, that children of all ages enjoy. Sentences are cut into two and the children are asked to re-form them to make a sensible statement. As they discuss the possibilities with other children, they may change their ideas and have to explain their thinking. If sentences are structured with care, children will need to think carefully whether there is more than one 'correct' answer. An example of Sentence Cards can be found in Activity 13, Can Can.

Sequencing

Sequencing involves putting a set of photographs, drawings, or sentences in a logical order, such as the stages in the Water Cycle. Having a tangible resource to move around is always helpful. Showing stages in a life cycle or a melting ice cube, for example, helps children develop and express their understanding of various aspects of the science that they study. Working together to complete sequences can also lead to further research and learning. If children are encouraged to justify their reasons for selecting the chosen sequence, then their skill in explanation will also be developed.

Drawings of observations, or photographs of a known area, could be used as an extended sequence to plot an interesting route around a habitat. An example of Sequencing can be found in Activity 21 (MS), Colourful Columns, Activity 2, Colourful Caterpillars, Activity 5, Veg Tops, and in Activity 11, Water Cycle Seedlings.

Sharing Memory

Using this strategy encourages children to work together as a team to remember and reproduce an image or diagram. The best results are achieved when the team supports and guides each member through the process. This collaborative activity can be used in other subjects such as geography (maps), history (family trees), art (portraits) and so on.

- Arrange children in small groups with an A3 sheet of paper and appropriate drawing materials.
- One member from each team is allowed to study a given image for a short time — perhaps 30 seconds. You may choose a digestive system, a flowering plant's reproductive organs or an illustrated table showing rocks, soils and their properties.
- Members return to their groups and draw what they have seen.

They can discuss this freely with their peers and quite soon a second team member from each group is called forward to see the image. They need to be told how many turns they will get before the drawing should be completed.

Allow groups to work without guidance the first time and compare each group's drawing with the original. Scanning the image and projecting it onto a screen allows you to point out to the whole class pertinent features that were done well or those which were entirely forgotten. Discuss with your class how their results would have improved if they had planned out together what each person should focus on when it was their turn to view. Sharing Memory forms Activity 7, Sharing Memory and another example can be found in Activity 18, Babysafe Brainsafe.

Splat!

This is a thinking skills version of *Bingo!* for teams to play. It can be organised in a number of ways. Teams of children select a 'splatter'. Organise a 'wall' made up of a variety of words or pictures. This 'wall' can be on a blackboard, a whiteboard, or it could be a set of words/pictures printed onto A4 paper and displayed on any flat surface. You read out a description or definition and whoever 'splats' their hand or thumb over the correct word or picture on the grid wins a point for their team. For example. *'This animal can fly … and it is very small … and it makes a buzzing noise when it flies. (Answer: bee)*

Children can be encouraged to explain their group's choice to the rest of the class. If other answers are chosen you could give the class time for discussion to see if they can reach agreement as to whether those answers can also be justified. An example of Splat! can be found in Activity 12, Heads and in Activity 19, Celebration Candles.

Stickers on Back

This strategy will liven up any potentially boring, static lessons, where diagrams are labelled with little challenge or use of brainpower. It also encourages children to think about the usefulness of the questions they ask.

Children are provided with a sticky label. The label contains, for example, the name of a body part. They stick the label onto the back of a partner, who is not allowed to see the word but has to discover which body part they are carrying. Using focused questions, the children attempt to find out the word on their label. Questions can only be answered with 'Yes', 'No' or 'Don't know.'

Challenge can be added by limiting the time allowed or the number of questions that can be asked. The strategy compels learners to think carefully about the questions they use and to collate the various answers that they are given. Stickers on Back forms the main part of Activity 1, Stick and Think and another example can be found in Activity 18, Babysafe Brainsafe.

Taboo!

You might like to demonstrate how Taboo is played before handing it over to the children. Working in groups of 4, one person is chosen to take a Taboo card from the pile. At the top of the card is a word in red. This is the Keyword, which the group will work together to try to guess. In addition, there is a set of Taboo words underneath the Keyword. The aim is for the group to guess the Keyword as quickly as possible.

Apart from the Keyword and Taboo words, the cardholder can use any words to describe the Keyword and help the group guess it.

Keyword: Potato - Taboo words: mash, chips, spuds, King Edwards

In the instance above, a child can't use any words that are written on the card but can say, 'It's a vegetable.' 'It grows under the ground.' ... and so on. An example of Taboo can be found in Activity 15 (MS), Ballooning.

Text to Table; Table to Text

This text restructuring activity encourages children to work together to analyse a given text closely and to put information into a prepared or an independently created table. Alternatively, the class can be given a table of facts and asked to write a few paragraphs of text on the information it contains. Children can be given a partially completed sheet and after some research, asked to add some more facts to the table. An example of Text to Table; Table to Text can be found in Activity 9 (MS), Habitat Boxes.

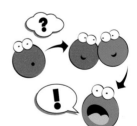

Think, Pair, Share

This strategy encourages children to think about and discuss their own and others' ideas. They spend a little time thinking about the task. Then each child joins another and the two children share their ideas. Finally two pairs come together to discuss and look for consensus.

If you have asked each pair to come up with two points, for example, you might ask the foursome to find three things to feed back to you and the rest of their classmates. Once again the children are supported in a small group, they can listen to other ideas and discuss before deciding on their answer. An example of Think, Pair, Share can be found in Activity 20, Comparative Circus.

Thinking Mat

A Thinking Mat is a good way to encourage children to talk together, listen to each other's ideas and reach agreement. For example, you might ask the class, "*What would a green plant need to grow successfully?*"

- Children write or draw their ideas on their own sheet of paper, without discussion.

- After a few minutes, small groups join together and are given a sheet of coloured paper, their Thinking Mat.

- In turn, children describe their ideas to the others.

- A scribe in the group jots down on the Thinking Mat the points where they agree.

- If the group can't agree on any particular point, it isn't added to the Thinking Mat. These points can be noted for further exploration and discussion later.

- Finally, the different Thinking Mats can be collected and compared. This can lead to more research or discussion across the class to support further learning.

This strategy allows children the opportunity to think, to share their ideas and to consider the ideas of others. It works very well as an introductory or review activity. An example of Thinking Mat can be found in Activity 20 (MS), Comparative Circus and in Activity 9, Habitat Boxes.

Thinking Quilt

Thinking quilts encourage children to examine scientific words closely for meaning and understanding. Using a grid containing words from a particular topic, such as digestion, the idea is to create as many sentences as possible using words that are adjacent to each other either vertically, horizontally or diagonally. They can also review the sentences from other groups to decide if they agree with their ideas and carry out further research to reach consensus. An example of Thinking Quilt can be found in Activity 7 (MS), Sharing Memory.

True False Statements

This simple strategy asks children to work together to decide if a statement is true or false. For example, 'All flowers have 6 petals.' They can use a variety of ways to show their decision such as thumbs up or down, a green or red card or note on a mini-whiteboard. This approach seems to appeal especially to those children who may be reluctant to commit themselves to an answer. Used at the beginning of a topic, the strategy will reveal a lot about their initial understanding and identify areas of uncertainty which can be the focus of further learning. An example of True False Statements can be found in Activity 18 (MS), Babysafe Brainsafe.

Venn Diagrams

The Venn Diagram is a type of graphic organiser used to compare, contrast and classify. Two or three circles overlap, with each circle containing examples of a particular set. The elements which are common to both sets are put in the space where the circles overlap, This is a useful, visual way of discussing similarities and differences and allows the children the opportunity to work together to explore and record their understanding.

Venn Diagrams help generate thinking and discussion and can provide evidence of children's thinking. An example of Venn Diagrams can be found in Activity 16 (MS), Sound Circus.

What Do We Know?

This strategy collates information to be discussed from different groups of children. Any areas of disagreement can lead into further investigation.

Arrange the class into groups of five and ask them to remember one thing about the topic under study. The first group member writes this idea very quickly at the top of a piece of paper. On a signal, after perhaps 10 seconds, the paper is folded over so that the sentence is not visible and passed to a second member of the group, who does the same. At the end of a minute or so the paper will contain five sentences about, for example, reversible and irreversible change. On your command, the paper is unfolded and the group reads and discusses the five sentences. Some ideas may come up more than once. During a class discussion, children can note whether anything important has been left out or forgotten. An example of What Do We Know? can be found in Activity 3, Slow Melt and in Activity 16, Sound Circus.

What's in the Box?

In this strategy the element of intrigue is used. A photograph, a small model, a drawing or a suitable living example of a plant or animal is placed in a box and the children challenged to work together to discover what it is. The number of questions asked can be unlimited or restricted to 20, one for each pair etc. Give a few clues, such as to where the object lives or whether it is an animal or a plant. Greater challenge comes when the children are given no clues at all. How many questions are needed to discover what's in the box?

Children then work together to identify questions about the plant or animal they could not answer to take their learning forward. An example of What's in the Box? can be found in Activity 9, Habitat Boxes.

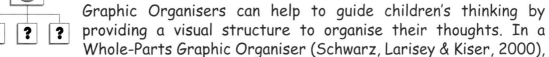

Whole-Parts Graphic Organiser

Graphic Organisers can help to guide children's thinking by providing a visual structure to organise their thoughts. In a Whole-Parts Graphic Organiser (Schwarz, Larisey & Kiser, 2000), the children need to think of the different parts of something and discuss what would happen if a single part were removed or missing.

The whole thing, the individual parts of the whole and what would happen if a part was missing create a visual structure that can produce a deeper understanding of form and function. For example, the children might think about a human body, its individual organs and the problems that missing one of those organs would produce. An example of a Whole-Parts Graphic Organiser can be found in Activity 11 (MS), Water Cycle Seedlings.

Yes, No, Maybe So

Yes/No/Maybe So is another version of True False statements. Children are asked to discuss a statement or a question and decide if it is true or false or if the answer is yes, no or maybe so.

For example, 'All insects have four legs.' Children can use a variety of ways to demonstrate their decisions, such as thumbs up, down or sideways, green, red or orange cards, small whiteboards and so on. When used at the beginning of a topic, this strategy reveals current understanding and can encourage further thinking and learning about the statement. An example of Yes/No/Maybe So can be found in Activity 13, Can Can.

STICK AND THINK

What it is

This fun activity results in immediate laughter whenever I use it. Each child has a sticky label on their back. They do not see what the label contains — in this instance the name of a body part. Their challenge is to ask questions to find out which body part they represent. Once a child has identified the part, they put their sticker on their front and try to find enough classmates to make a 'working' body. You could also try parts of a plant, a circuit, or other objects, systems or processes.

This activity helps children to learn about parts of the body and their relationship to each other. It develops thinking and questioning skills, and scientific vocabulary.

Resources

You need:

- ☐ sticky labels each containing one word, such as: *head, arm, leg, knee, shoulder, eye, ear, lips, teeth, toes*. To make it more demanding you can use words such as: *lungs, stomach, heart, large intestine, brain, spine, humerus, tibia*. Parts such as eyebrows, teeth, fingernails and joints prove the most difficult to identify

- ☐ if children are to make a 'working' body, remember to include more than one sticker for leg, arm, hand etc.

 Children should walk, not run.
Some fabrics can be damaged by sticky label adhesive.

How to use it

One person on each table distributes the labels face down. Everyone looks at their word but keeps it to themselves. Then each child fixes their label to the back of someone near to them.

Make the rules clear before the activity begins. You can limit the time or limit the number of questions asked. For example:

- The aim is to find which body part is written on your label.
- You can move around the room to ask questions to help you. Choose your questions carefully.
- You can ask up to 15 people.
- The answer to a question can only be 'Yes', 'No' or 'I don't know'.
- Once you've worked it out or asked 15 questions sit down.

The more children understand about the human body, the more detailed and specific questions are likely to be. They can move from simple questions about position or features to more complex questions about the function of organs.

- Ask the children to consider how some questions provided more information than others. For example, is 'Am I a leg?' as useful a question as 'Am I part of the digestive system?'

Key questions

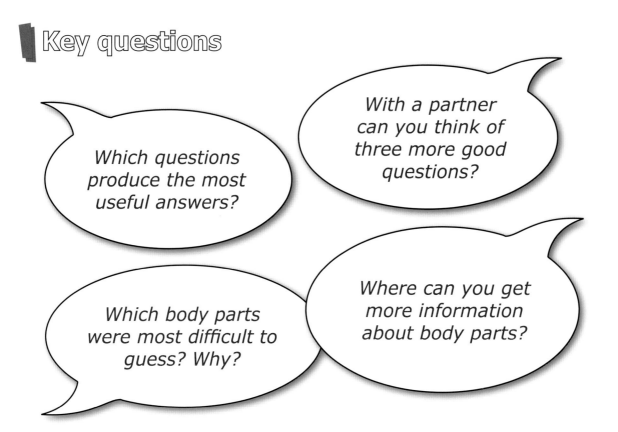

Which questions produce the most useful answers?

With a partner can you think of three more good questions?

Which body parts were most difficult to guess? Why?

Where can you get more information about body parts?

Extending the activity

There is more information about this strategy in the Strategies chapter at the beginning of the book.

Divide the children into groups of three. Give them the Listening Trios Report. This activity gives them an opportunity to learn more about working well as trios. They need to think carefully about the trios conversation and how they could improve what Jake, Izzy and Rahul did. Afterwards, they take on the role of the *Talker*, the *Questioner* or the *Recorder* and carry out their own trios using the Listening Trios Guidelines. The Report and Guidelines worksheets are **on the CD**.

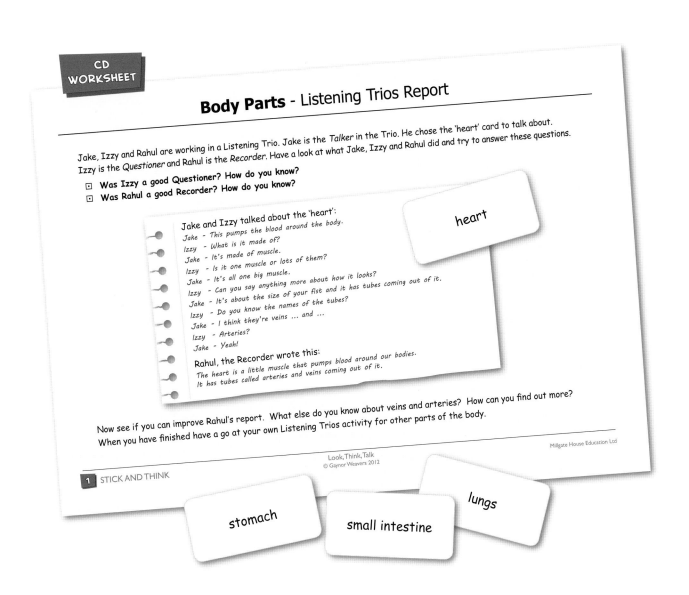

CD WORKSHEET

Body Parts - Listening Trios Report

Jake, Izzy and Rahul are working in a Listening Trio. Jake is the *Talker* in the Trio. He chose the 'heart' card to talk about. Izzy is the *Questioner* and Rahul is the *Recorder*. Have a look at what Jake, Izzy and Rahul did and try to answer these questions.

- ☑ Was Izzy a good Questioner? How do you know?
- ☑ Was Rahul a good Recorder? How do you know?

Jake and Izzy talked about the 'heart':

Jake - This pumps the blood around the body.
Izzy - What is it made of?
Jake - It's made of muscle.
Izzy - Is it one muscle or lots of them?
Jake - It's all one big muscle.
Izzy - Can you say anything more about how it looks?
Jake - It's about the size of your fist and it has tubes coming out of it.
Izzy - Do you know the names of the tubes?
Jake - I think they're veins ... and ...
Izzy - Arteries?
Jake - Yeah!

heart

Rahul, the Recorder wrote this:
The heart is a little muscle that pumps blood around our bodies. It has tubes called arteries and veins coming out of it.

Now see if you can improve Rahul's report. What else do you know about veins and arteries? How can you find out more?
When you have finished have a go at your own Listening Trios activity for other parts of the body.

Millgate House Education Ltd

Look, Think, Talk
© Gaynor Weavers 2012

1 STICK AND THINK

stomach

small intestine

lungs

Post-it Challenge

Children work in small groups. Within a time limit they jot on Post-its three things they know about a specified organ or part of the body, such as the heart. Call groups forward to the board to stick their Post-its around the targeted word. You might want to group the responses into position, structure, function, importance to the body, and so on. Read each note aloud and see if the class agrees. Encourage them to do more thinking and research where there is disagreement or uncertainty. Subsequently, children can research and compare the function of body parts of other animals.

Design & Technology / ICT

Research using the Internet or the library can help children discover relevant information about the human body's structure. Challenge groups to make large, card models of the human body. Organ shapes can be made as flaps, with the function of the organ explained underneath. (This will link to the Post-it challenge above.)

Maths / ICT

Ask children to read a couple of paragraphs of text outlining an activity. (See example below.) Can they create a graph on paper or computer, with suitable labelling, to show what is happening to Jamie's heart rate?

Jamie leaves the house and strolls towards school. He sees the clock above the Police Station and realises that he is almost late! He runs the rest of the way to school. Teacher tells him the clock has been stuck at 8.55 a.m. for several days. It is only 8.40 a.m. so Jamie can sit and have a chat with his friends in the classroom.

History & RE

Children can be surprised by what our ancestors believed about the function of different parts of the body. For example, the heart and stomach were once thought to control emotions. Burial rites of ancient civilisations showed how organs were valued — the Egyptians stored most of the organs of wealthy individuals in jars for the afterlife.

Looking for evidence of thinking and learning

In this activity children have the opportunity to:

✓ use and explore scientific vocabulary of external, visible parts such as head, nose, eyebrows, wrist, or internal organs like lungs, heart, kidneys, etc.

✓ develop their ability to use research

✓ extend their knowledge of body parts and their functions, such as breathing, respiration, digestion, excretion, movement, etc.

✓ consider the usefulness of questions

✓ think about constructing clearly focused questions

✓ listen carefully to, analyse, record and present given information

They can do this by:

✓ recalling information and asking questions during the Stickers activity and Listening trios

✓ listening carefully during Listening trios and Post-it challenge

✓ comparing their notes with other Listening trios

✓ creating models of the body

✓ creating graphs of human activity

✓ researching historical views of the functions of the body

You should see evidence of their thinking and learning in:

✓ the questions they ask during the main Stickers activity

✓ the spoken and written outcomes from the Listening trios activity

✓ the information that they produce during the Post-it challenge

✓ the body models they produce

✓ the outcomes of their research from books or the Internet

✓ the labelled graphs that they draw

✓ the ideas they express, in writing or orally, when they reflect on their own learning

What children do

*Listening Trio
at work*

Reviewing the learning

? How did thinking about the questions before you asked them help you in the sticker activity?

? What makes a good Talker, Questioner or Recorder? How well did you do in each role? Did working in a group improve your learning?

? What did you learn about the human body that you didn't know before?

? How many body parts did you find that you could not survive without?

COLOURFUL CATERPILLARS

What it is

In this lively activity small pieces of coloured wool, representing caterpillars, are scattered over the school field and/or shrubs. Children investigate which colour of caterpillar is most easy or difficult to locate. If the school does not have easy access to a green field, a large piece of fabric laid out in the school hall is a suitable substitute, although wool colours and the amount of time allowed may need to be adjusted, as this is less of a challenge for the children.

This activity helps children to learn about the role of adaptation in both plants and animals. It can be used as a precursor or a follow-up to work on food chains.

Resources

You need:

☐ a collection of wool strands, each about 4 cm long in a variety of colours and shades (there should be the same number of strands of each colour)

☐ Tally Chart 1 so children can record how many colours of each type were found. It is on the CD.

 Explore your school field beforehand and check for potential hazards, such as animal waste, broken glass and so on. Provide disposable gloves for the children or ensure children understand the need for effective hygiene and hand-washing after the activity. (Child size disposable gloves are available from equipment suppliers.)

How to use it

Arrange the class into groups of 4 or 5.

Each group needs Tally Chart 1 and a team member to record the results — the group recorder. (Tally Chart 1 is **on the CD**)

Explain that a large number of very hungry, colourful, 'woolly caterpillars' have invaded the school field and other green areas. It's important to collect as many caterpillars as possible before they eat all the green leaves around school.

The group recorder needs to make sure that all the different types of caterpillar found are noted on the tally chart worksheet.

Every two minutes blow a whistle to stop the search. The group's recorder makes a note of the number of each colour found by the group and passes it to the class recorder. Allow the groups a few moments to discuss their results and plan their next search. A whistle signals the start of the next two-minute search. The recorders can be changed regularly to allow everyone the opportunity to have a go. The total time allowed will depend on the size of your field and the number of strands used.

Key questions

Which colours were easiest to find? Which did you find first?

Did you find more of one colour than the others? Why do you think this is?

Where do green caterpillars normally live? How does their colour help them to survive?

What do you think would happen if all the green caterpillars suddenly became bright pink?

Extending the activity

STRATEGY: *News Report*

There is more information about this strategy in the Strategies chapter at the beginning of the book.

Give each group the News Report. Tell your class that gardeners and farmers have noticed, over the past few weeks, that the Small Cabbage White caterpillars have been changing colour from green to pink. Ask your class to read the report and talk about it. Who do they agree with and why? What do they think should be done?

Share ideas across the class and try to resolve any disagreements. Finally they write a similar news report for a different animal, using the format on the worksheet and share the reports with each other. The News Report is **on the CD**.

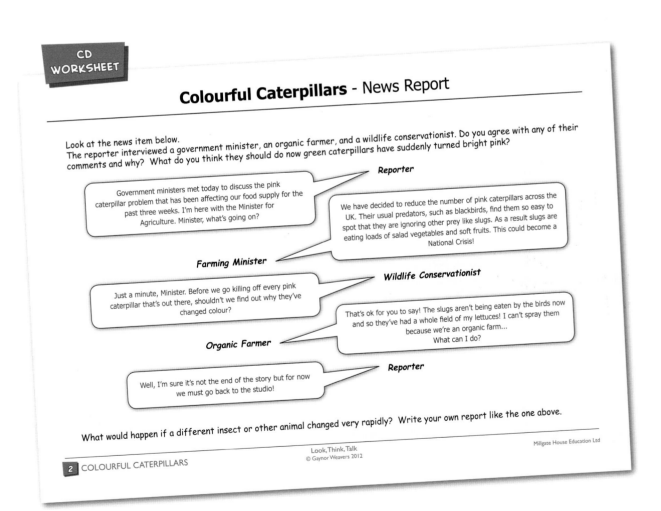

CD WORKSHEET

Colourful Caterpillars - News Report

Look at the news item below.
The reporter interviewed a government minister, an organic farmer, and a wildlife conservationist. Do you agree with any of their comments and why? What do you think they should do now green caterpillars have suddenly turned bright pink?

Reporter

Government ministers met today to discuss the pink caterpillar problem that has been affecting our food supply for the past three weeks. I'm here with the Minister for Agriculture. Minister, what's going on?

We have decided to reduce the number of pink caterpillars across the UK. Their usual predators, such as blackbirds, find them so easy to spot that they are ignoring other prey like slugs. As a result slugs are eating loads of salad vegetables and soft fruits. This could become a National Crisis!

Farming Minister

Wildlife Conservationist

Just a minute, Minister. Before we go killing off every pink caterpillar that's out there, shouldn't we find out why they've changed colour?

That's ok for you to say! The slugs aren't being eaten by the birds now and so they've had a whole field of my lettuces! I can't spray them because we're an organic farm...
What can I do?

Organic Farmer

Reporter

Well, I'm sure it's not the end of the story but for now we must go back to the studio!

What would happen if a different insect or other animal changed very rapidly? Write your own report like the one above.

Look, Think, Talk
© Gaynor Weavers 2012

Millgate House Education Ltd

2 COLOURFUL CATERPILLARS

Sequencing

Give the children sets of cards containing arrow symbols and the names of plants and animals. Ask them to identify different food chains. Groups or pairs can compare their findings. Where appropriate, some children can compile a food web.

Just a Minute

Children research one caterpillar from a given list. Classmates ask questions to discover which caterpillar has been chosen. An identification guide could be given to pupils at the start. Alternatively, groups can research and pool information as in the Jigsawing activity below.

Jigsawing

In groups of 5 or 6, each child is challenged to find out one thing about several selected butterflies. For example — where they live; what they eat; what they look like; the different stages of their life cycles. Children researching the same feature work together before returning to their original groups to share what they have found out.

Maths

This activity lends itself well to lots of maths activities such as data handling, data analysis and graphing of findings. Graphs and graphing programs can be used to display results from the caterpillar survey. (See Tally Chart 2 **on the CD**.) Children can also calculate percentages of each colour found in a given time. In addition, problem solving activities could be devised using work on probability.

History, Design & Technology

If children research Darwin's work on birds and adaptation in the Galapagos islands, they can make card 'beaks', which can be used to pick up seeds, berries etc. They can then explain their findings.

Looking for evidence of thinking and learning

In this activity children have the opportunity to:

✓ extend their understanding of adaptation and survival

✓ learn how to pattern seek

✓ develop their skills of displaying data from their investigation and use it to calculate percentages and discuss probabilities

✓ use and explore the meaning of scientific vocabulary such as adaptation, camouflage, habitat, predator, prey, etc.

✓ learn more about media reporting

✓ develop their understanding of food chains

✓ develop their skills of gathering information from a range of sources

They can do this by:

✓ investigating how some wools are better 'camouflaged' than others

✓ using their findings to produce tables, graphs and probabilities and to calculate percentages

✓ talking about and composing exciting News reports of unusual environmental events

✓ using a Sequencing activity to create food chains

✓ taking part in Just a minute and Jigsawing activities

✓ exploring the work of Darwin on the Galapagos Islands

You should see evidence of their thinking and learning in:

✓ what they say to you and each other about adaptation

✓ their explanations of the importance of colour to the survival of some caterpillars

✓ how they handle and analyse data

✓ what they say about News reports and the content of the News reports they write

✓ the food chains they produce in the Sequencing activity

✓ their research findings into Charles Darwin and animal adaptation

What children do

Completing Sequences

Reviewing the learning

? What surprised you about searching for the 'caterpillars'? Were the results what you expected?

? How did the sequencing activity help you understand food chains?

? How can you use what you have learned to think of ways that other animals use colour to help them to survive?

? What have you learned about how caterpillars adapt to their environment that you didn't know before?

SLOW MELT

What it is

This fascinating activity allows children to watch a variety of materials as they change *slowly* during heating. Classmates can talk to each other and make notes about their observations. Small zigzag books of drawn and annotated observations help children consider the processes that they have seen.

This activity helps children to learn about physical and chemical changes in materials and gives them the opportunity to observe reversible and irreversible changes.

Resources

Each pair or small group needs:
- ☐ a tea light and stand in a tray of sand
- ☐ small foil dishes to hold the materials
- ☐ safety glasses
- ☐ approximatly half a tsp each of substances such as chocolate, ice cubes, cheese, butter, bread, apple, jelly cubes etc.

A fire blanket should be readily available.

Tie back long hair and roll up sleeves to prevent contact with the naked flame.

Extinguish the flame *gently* - blowing vigorously can propel hot wax out of the container. Metal dishes, tea light stands and heated substances should not be touched with unprotected hands.

Test substances beforehand to ensure they're safe. Safety goggles should be used when heating substances high in sugar or fat as they may 'spit'.

How to use it

Talk through the activity and demonstrate clearly all safety measures. The procedure will be as follows:

- Place the substance in the dish above the lit tea light in the stand. (Warn children to stop heating a substance if it begins to bubble in the dish. Children can try to predict what will happen if you continue to heat chocolate and other substances, but this is best done as a demonstration.)

- Observe carefully what happens, and record any changes noticed using sight, sound and smell. (Warn children not to get too close.)

- Allow dishes to cool slowly to see whether each change is reversible or irreversible.

- Compare several substances. **Warn children not to pick up recently heated dishes or tea light stands**.

  N.B. If you give everyone the same substance to study initially, you can address the same questions to the whole class. For example:
  - *Is it melting at the top or the bottom?*
  - *How much solid material is left?*
  - *Can you smell anything?*

- Finally children make zigzag books to record what they have found out.

Key questions

Which substances showed reversible changes? Which were irreversible?

What have you learned by looking at others people's drawings?

What difference does it make if you heat things for different amounts of time?

Was there anything that surprised you?

Extending the activity

There is more information about this strategy in the Strategies chapter at the beginning of the book.

Give children the Concept Sentences. They cut out the words and try to create sentences with them. The words include a selection of nouns, adjectives and connectives to make sentence construction easier. Children can add their own words to the sentences. Differences between sentences are shared and used as a stimulus for new learning. The Concept Sentences are **on the CD**.

STRATEGY:
Concept Sentences

? ! ?   HEAVY
HARD   SQUISHY
SOFT

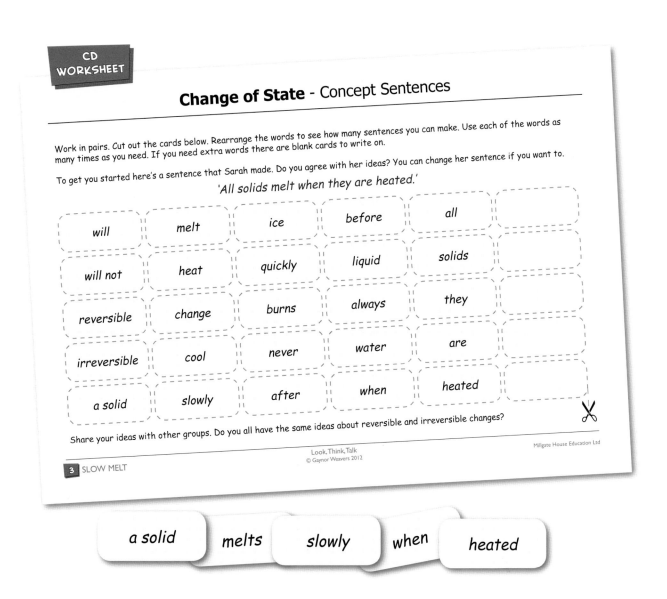

CD WORKSHEET

Change of State - Concept Sentences

Work in pairs. Cut out the cards below. Rearrange the words to see how many sentences you can make. Use each of the words as many times as you need. If you need extra words there are blank cards to write on.

To get you started here's a sentence that Sarah made. Do you agree with her ideas? You can change her sentence if you want to.

'All solids melt when they are heated.'

will	melt	ice	before	all
will not	heat	quickly	liquid	solids
reversible	change	burns	always	they
irreversible	cool	never	water	are
a solid	slowly	after	when	heated

Share your ideas with other groups. Do you all have the same ideas about reversible and irreversible changes?

Look, Think, Talk
© Gaynor Weavers 2012

Millgate House Education Ltd

3 SLOW MELT

a solid   melts   slowly   when   heated

Extending the activity cont.

Posters

Children design Posters that describe materials so incredible that people haven't yet realised that they were needed! For example, ice lollies that won't melt in the sunshine or bread that instantly turns to toast.

What Do We Know?

Ask the class to arrange themselves into groups and think of all that they know about reversible and irreversible change for 3 minutes. Then they can play 'What Do We Know?' This collates information from each group that can be discussed. Any areas of disagreement can lead to further research.

Design & Technology, Language, Art & ICT

DESIGN & TECH

LANGUAGE

ART & ICT

This activity and the Concept Sentences strategy help to develop science vocabulary and language skills and encourage further research. Planning, making and decorating the small zigzag books uses both literacy and art skills. Alternatively, the books could be designed and created using a computer program.

Maths & Geography

MATHS

GEOGRAPHY

The children produce bar graphs to compare rates of melting in various materials or line graphs for rates of melting of different volumes of ice.

Plan views of the sequence of how the substances melt are recorded in the zigzag books. These can be used to reinforce the skill of drawing plans in both maths and geography.

Looking for evidence of thinking and learning

In this activity children have the opportunity to:

- ✓ extend their knowledge of materials and melting
- ✓ learn how to be safe when carrying out practical science
- ✓ use and explore the meaning of scientific vocabulary such as solid, liquid, melt, dissolve, reversible, irreversible, permanent, etc.
- ✓ learn how to observe over time
- ✓ develop their skills of producing bar charts or line graphs
- ✓ become more confident to explore creative ideas

They can do this by:

- ✓ observing and recording the effect of heat on various materials
- ✓ heating materials safely using simple apparatus
- ✓ creating sentences about reversible and irreversible change using the Concept sentences strategy
- ✓ making predictions about outcomes
- ✓ graphing data from melting ice activities
- ✓ creating Posters, solving problems and writing letters to imaginary individuals
- ✓ making zigzag books

You should see evidence of their thinking and learning in:

- ✓ what they say to you and each other about their observations
- ✓ their spoken or written comments about heating materials safely and what they do
- ✓ their written or spoken comments about what happens when they heat the materials
- ✓ the sentences they create in the Concept sentences activity and what they say about them
- ✓ the graphs that they produce
- ✓ the Posters that they create
- ✓ the zigzag books that they create

What children do

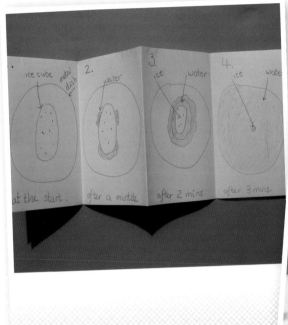

A completed zigzag book

Creating Concept Sentences

Reviewing the learning

? Can you explain how observing things melting helps you understand more about how things change?

? How did creating a zigzag book and annotating your observations help you focus on what was happening?

? How would you explain your poster about changes to a younger class?

? What have you learned about how things change when they are heated that you didn't know before?

EAT YOUR WORDS

What it is

This is guaranteed to be a popular activity! Children design and create an item such as a make-believe menu for an animal's 'restaurant'. The twist in the tail to this activity is that all elements of their card or poster are edible, including the rice paper on which the design is produced so, children can literally eat their own words! If other topics, such as food groups, invertebrates, food chains or plants are chosen, then products like an invitation, a card, an advert or a seed packet can be made.

This activity helps children to learn about predators, prey, food chains and feeding relationships, while writing for a particular purpose.

Resources

Each group needs:

☐ a range of resources for making edible cards. Cook shops are a good source for most of the following: rice paper, fondant or moulding icing, icing pens, icing sugar, preformed shapes of icing, liquorice laces, candy sticks, jelly sweets, food colouring etc.

☐ access to information sources about animals' diets and feeding relationships.

 If the products are to be eaten refer to your school's hygiene policy. Remind children of all aspects of personal hygiene, such as careful hand and nail cleaning, rolling up sleeves and tying hair back. Use domestic disinfectant sprays to keep work surfaces clean. In addition, check any allergies that children may have.

How to use it

- Start the task with a problem such as, *'There's a new restaurant for animals but the menus haven't arrived. What sort of foods would your chosen animal eat? Be creative with the names of each course.'*

- Show them some examples of menus if you feel that they need help to develop their ideas before making their own menus.

- Let children see the resources and discuss their suitability. Remind them of health and safety measures.

- Tell the children that their menus need to be based on what animals actually eat. Highlight the information that can be gleaned from text and accompanying pictures.

- Warn the children they only get one go at making the real thing, so they need to design the product on paper first.

- Children can annotate their designs to ensure they have planned all of their requirements before they begin. These designs can be kept and displayed, along with photographs of the final products, as a record of their ideas.

- Children can evaluate each other's designs and research any areas of uncertainty before they make the final product.

- Photograph the completed products before finally allowing the children to eat them.

Key questions

How did you find out what this animal needs to live successfully?

How accurate is the information on your menu? How do you know?

Would you swap places with this animal? Why?

Extending the activity

There is more information about this strategy in the Strategies chapter at the beginning of the book.

Give the children the Animals KWHL Grid. This worksheet is designed to give children experience of KWHL Grids before doing their own. Challenge them to reflect on what Helena and Maya have done. Encourage them to be critical.

When they have done this discuss with them how to create their own KWHL Grid before they move on to the next part of the activity using the Blank KWHL Grid. The KWHL Grids are **on the CD**.

CD WORKSHEET

Animals - KWHL Grid

We are finding out about .... *Sharks* ....

This is Helena and Maya's KWHL Grid. They have been researching sharks. Have they answered all their questions? Are there any other ways of finding out information that they could have used? They are not sure if all their ideas are correct. You can change what they have written if you want to.

What do we think we Know about ...*Sharks*... already?	What do we Want to find out about ...*Sharks*..?	How will we find out?	What have we Learnt about ...*Sharks*..?
They are dangerous carnivores.	How many people a year do they eat?	Internet	They are not always dangerous to humans. Only three shark species; the Great White, Tiger, and Bull Sharks have been reported to attack people.
They have lots of teeth.	What do they eat?		There have been no attacks in this country since 1847, but two fishermen had bites while they were removing hooks from the mouths of sharks they'd caught.
They live in warm places.	Are there sharks in every sea and ocean?		Sharks attack less than 100 people a year in the whole world.
			What they eat depends on what type of shark they are. They all eat meat, and some eat tiny plants and animals called plankton.

Now use the Blank KWHL Grid to research your own animal. Don't forget to start with what they eat.

Look, Think, Talk
© Gaynor Weavers 2012

Millgate House Education Ltd

4 EAT YOUR WORDS

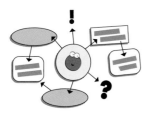

Mind Map

Another way to develop their knowledge and understanding is to ask the children to create a Mind Map. In the example overleaf, they have been looking at sharks so their Mind Maps can have radiating branches showing where sharks live, what they eat, their teeth, the types of shark found near the UK and beyond and so on. Mind Maps can be colourfully illustrated to aid thinking.

Expert Witness

Children become the expert on their particular animal. Their classmates can ask questions and any that cannot be answered can be recorded for further research.

Geography

Pairs explore the habitat where particular animals live and identify their positions in the world using world atlases, maps, globes or the Internet. They then join with another pair and compare the habitats of their chosen animals looking at differences in climate, local flora and fauna, topography etc.

Language, Art, Music

This activity has numerous links to the language and arts curricula. The scenario chosen sets the context for any tasks undertaken. For example, if a shark's menu is the focus, children can plan a shark's birthday party and create party items such as invitations, food, drinks, cards, placemats and guest name labels. Songs and poems can be written to perform at the party itself.

Looking for evidence of thinking and learning

In this activity children have the opportunity to:

✓ use and explore the meaning of scientific vocabulary, such as predator, prey, producer, consumer, habitat, food chain, feeding relationships, carnivore, herbivore, omnivore, decomposers, nutrients, energy, etc.

✓ develop their ability to use research

✓ develop an awareness of the differences between the habitats where different animals live

✓ develop their skills of designing and annotating plans and using ideas creatively

✓ develop confidence in answering their classmates' questions about a topic they have researched

✓ develop their understanding of how to make and evaluate a product

They can do this by:

✓ designing and creating an edible menu

✓ evaluating each other's plans

✓ using books or the Internet to find out about what animals eat

✓ using and completing a KWHL grid or Mind map

✓ acting as an Expert witness

✓ finding out about habitats using maps, atlases, world globes and other information sources

✓ making party resources

You should see evidence of their thinking and learning in:

✓ what they say to you and each other about their research

✓ the menus and the annotated plans they create

✓ their completed KWHL grids and Mind maps

✓ the answers they give their classmates as an Expert witness

✓ how they use geographical resources such as globes, maps and atlases

✓ the party resources that they produce

What children do

A completed KWHL Grid

Reviewing the learning

? How did making an edible menu help you show what you've learnt?

? How did doing the design first help you plan your menu?

? How did making a KWHL grid help you to learn about what animals eat?

? What have you learned about feeding relationships that you didn't know before?

VEG TOPS

What it is

Although we encourage children to germinate seeds in primary school, they rarely see other ways in which plants begin to grow.

This delightful activity allows children to see how vegetables can propagate from growing tips. It ensures that children look closely at cut vegetable tops as they sprout leaves and even develop flowers. They talk about how and why the leaves and flowers are developing and think about the other changes that may be seen over time. The term 'vegetable' in common use generally means the leaf, stem or root of a plant. You might like to compare and contrast this with seeds and fruits.

This activity helps children to learn about plant growth and propagation.

Resources

You need:

☑ a variety of vegetables, such as carrots, parsnips, beetroot, turnips and potatoes - some of which show the beginnings of growth

☑ small saucers or dishes to hold the vegetable tops

☑ suitable knives to remove the vegetable tops.

 If children use the knives independently, reminders should be given about how to handle them safely. Ensure that children do not touch any mould that may appear on the vegetable tops or the surrounding water. Children should wash their hands after handling vegetables.

How to use it

Ask children to observe, handle and draw the different vegetables. They can discuss similarities and differences such as shape, size, colour, taste, weight, country of origin and so on.

Show them a carrot top that you have been growing for a few days (instructions below) and ask them to talk about and draw what they think will happen to other vegetables that are treated in the same way.

Provide each group with a selection of vegetables and, if children are mature enough, ask them to remove about 1 cm from the tops of the vegetables using a knife. Each top should be placed in a dish of shallow water. (N.B. If water covers the whole top it will rot.)

Leave the dishes in a warm and light place. Top up the water as it evaporates. Ask children to record any changes that happen over a period of weeks.

Although they often expect them to be the same, children will see that the sprouting leaves of different vegetables vary in shape, size and colour.

Key questions

How long was it before you saw any change?

Did it change in the way that you expected?

What did you notice when you compared the different types of vegetable after one week, two weeks and so on?

Did each type of vegetable change in the same way?

Extending the activity

STRATEGY:

Jigsawing

There is more information about this strategy in the Strategies chapter at the beginning of the book.

Divide your class into groups of four or five, and get them to select a vegetable for study. Each group member then chooses a Task Card from the Jigsawing worksheet. All the children who are looking at the same question, for example planting seeds, form a new group. They support each other in researching their questions using a variety of sources. After a given time, they rejoin their home group to share their findings. Finally, they create a display about their vegetable — for example annotated posters or a PowerPoint display. The Jigsawing worksheet is **on the CD**.

CD WORKSHEET

Plant Growth - Jigsawing

Meesha and Connie's class have been growing the tops of vegetables. They have collected lots of questions about growing vegetables and put them on cards. Your challenge is to help them to answer their questions. Here are their questions.

- What is the name and variety of your vegetable?
- Which part of the plant is harvested for eating - leaf, stem, root, flower?
- Can you eat the other parts?

- Does your vegetable flower?
- Is it possible to collect seeds from your plant?
- What does the 'yield' of each plant mean?

- Can you find some simple recipes for cooking your vegetable?
- Which vitamins does your vegetable contain?
- Is your vegetable suitable for freezing?

- How soon will the seeds germinate?
- What does your growing plant need to grow healthily?
- What conditions do the seeds need to germinate?

- What do the seeds of your plant look like?
- How and where should they be planted?

- What is the life cycle of your vegetable?

In your group choose one of the vegetables that you have grown. Each person choose one of the sets of questions to answer. Find all the other people in the class who have chosen the same set of questions. Work together in your new groups to help each other find the answers to that set of questions for your own group's vegetable. You might have different vegetables.

Go back to your home group, when your teacher tells you, so that you can all share your research. Gather together everything you have found about growing your vegetable. What do you think is the best way to share what you have found out?

Look, Think, Talk
© Gaynor Weavers 2012

Millgate House Education Ltd

5 VEG TOPS

Sequencing

Ask the children to regularly photograph their growing vegetable from different distances and angles. When the individual images are printed onto card, classmates can be challenged to show a life cycle of that vegetable.

Just a Minute

Children choose one vegetable from a given list. Classmates ask questions to discover which vegetable has been chosen. They research their choice and talk about it for a full minute. An information booklet can be given to all children at the start.

LANGUAGE

DESIGN & TECH

Language and Design & Technology

The research done on individual vegetables can be collated into illustrated information booklets suitable for a given audience — for example, younger children. The addition of a quiz, puzzle or recipe at the end of the booklet makes it even more attractive to other children.

Seeds and seed packets for fantastical plants with strange, edible parts that give magical powers can be designed and made.

MATHS & ICT

Maths & ICT

If children follow up the lesson by growing vegetables from seed, they can produce graphs and time lapse films of the growing plants. Any produce to be eaten can also be measured and weighed. Finally, vegetables can be cooked following simple recipes.

Looking for evidence of thinking and learning

In this activity children have the opportunity to:

✓ extend their understanding of plant life cycles and the conditions needed for plant growth

✓ use and explore the meaning of scientific vocabulary such as seed, root, shoot, leaf, fruit, flower, germinate, compost, life cycle, etc.

✓ develop their understanding of how to use secondary sources to answer questions

✓ develop their understanding of how to communicate ideas to different audiences

✓ develop their ability to record growth and change data into graphs

✓ develop an understanding of how to record changes using IT

✓ understand the relationship between growing plants and the food we eat

They can do this by:

✓ growing and observing vegetable tops and seeds in various conditions

✓ photographing and Sequencing photographs of plant life cycles

✓ taking part in the Just a minute game

✓ creating information booklets about a chosen vegetable

✓ designing seed packets for fantastical plants

✓ producing short time lapse films of seed growth

✓ preparing and cooking simple vegetable dishes

You should see evidence of their thinking and learning in:

✓ what they say to you and each other about growing vegetables

✓ the annotated drawings that they produce

✓ their Sequencing and Just a minute activities

✓ the vocabulary that they use in their annotated booklets

✓ how they take measurements and the graphs that they create

✓ their designs for seed packets for strange plants

✓ what they say about how the vegetable dishes were produced

What children do

Recording changes in radish tops

Reviewing the learning

? What surprised you about how the vegetable tops grew?

? What other ways of growing plants do you know about now?

? How did working with other children in the Jigsaw activity help you understand about the growth of plants?

? What have you learned about plant growth that you didn't know before?

MARBLE DROP

What it is

In this absorbing activity children observe, measure and compare the rates of fall of a single marble through columns of various household liquids. Children can plan their investigation as a fair test and, once they have experimented with three or four liquids, they can be given the challenge of creating a timer for a specific purpose.

This activity helps children to learn more about the nature of everyday liquids.

Resources

Each group needs:

- a selection of safe, transparent liquids of varying thicknesses (viscosity), such as water, fruit squash, cooking oils, syrup, washing up liquid, shampoo, vinegar and so on
- measuring cylinders at least 100 ml in volume. The longer the tube the more time the children have to observe and collect results
- stopwatches or watches with second hands
- absorbent towels or cloths in case of spills.

 Discuss the potential dangers of putting marbles or liquids in their mouths. Ensure all liquids used are safe for children. Children should be told that they must not drink or mix household chemicals because doing either of these can be very dangerous. Reinforce safety procedures for liquid splashed into eyes. Children can wear safety glasses if appropriate.

How to use it

Encourage children to explore the liquids in their containers. Let them stir them, tip them upside down and discuss colour, smell, transparency and viscosity. This gives them an opportunity to talk about and identify the differences between the liquids.

Explain to the children that they are shortly going to be given a challenge. To do the challenge they need to explore how quickly things (e.g. a marble) fall in different liquids. Encourage children to discuss how the activity can be carried out as a fair test and to make decisions about what to do. Extend the investigation by dropping objects of different shapes and sizes (e.g. lumps of plasticine) through a chosen liquid. Now challenge children to use this information to make a liquid timer.

Results gained when using very large measuring cylinders may surprise you. One marble took 16 minutes to complete its fall through a particular bubble bath. Groups or individuals can create a table and bar chart, using IT if appropriate. Children can research the use of different liquids and how liquids of different thicknesses are used in cooling, lubrication, etc.

Key questions

Now that you've tried your liquids, can you predict how long the marble will take to fall through this new liquid?

How are these liquids the same? How are they different?

Why does it matter if a liquid is very runny or very thick? When would it make a difference?

Extending the activity

There is more information about this strategy in the Strategies chapter at the beginning of the book.

Give the children the Odd One Out worksheet. Talk through with them what to do. Explain to them that there is often more than one solution to an Odd One Out problem. Encourage children to share their solution with their classmates and justify their choice. Children should try to find ways of resolving any disagreements. The worksheet is **on the CD**.

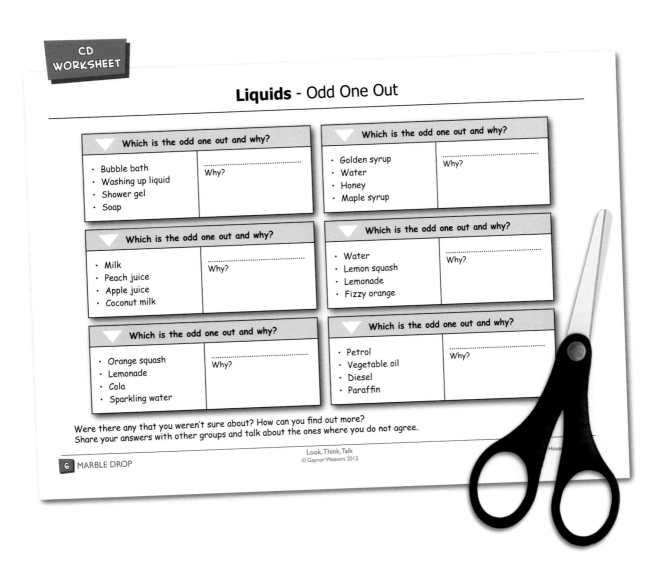

CD WORKSHEET

Liquids - Odd One Out

Which is the odd one out and why?

- Bubble bath
- Washing up liquid
- Shower gel
- Soap

Why?

Which is the odd one out and why?

- Golden syrup
- Water
- Honey
- Maple syrup

Why?

Which is the odd one out and why?

- Milk
- Peach juice
- Apple juice
- Coconut milk

Why?

Which is the odd one out and why?

- Water
- Lemon squash
- Lemonade
- Fizzy orange

Why?

Which is the odd one out and why?

- Orange squash
- Lemonade
- Cola
- Sparkling water

Why?

Which is the odd one out and why?

- Petrol
- Vegetable oil
- Diesel
- Paraffin

Why?

Were there any that you weren't sure about? How can you find out more?
Share your answers with other groups and talk about the ones where you do not agree.

Look, Think, Talk
© Gaynor Weavers 2012

6 MARBLE DROP

Classifying and Grouping

Groups investigate the liquids and complete a table, showing properties of the liquids. They can consider transparency, thickness, colour, scent, use and so on. Once this data is analysed, branching databases can be produced.

MATHS | Maths

While solving this problem, children select suitable mathematical equipment, using it accurately to measure time, while recording results using decimal notation if appropriate. They create a graph showing the results from a range of liquids.

ART | Art

The range of available liquids is wide and appealing. Following the activity above, challenge learners to create a spectrum of colours.

DESIGN & TECH | Design & Technology

Children are asked to generate ideas for a device that will drop marbles into a range of liquids at the same time and from the same height. Their own and classmates' devices are reviewed and constructive feedback given. Children can be asked to use liquids to make a set of timers — e.g. for 2, 5, 10 and 30 seconds. How well do their timers compare with manufactured or electronic timers?

DANCE DRAMA | Dance and Drama

Children use dance or drama to communicate ideas about how liquids of different viscosities move or pour.

Looking for evidence of thinking and learning

In this activity children have the opportunity to:

✓ extend their knowledge of the behaviour of everyday liquids such as drinks, toiletries, detergents, foods and so on

✓ use and exlore the meaning of scientific vocabulary such as liquid, flow, runny, viscous, volume, sinking, transparency, etc.

✓ develop their ability to describe and explain similarities and differences between liquids

✓ consolidate their ability to devise a fair test investigation, using simple equipment and measuring time

✓ develop their skills of making and evaluating products

They can do this by:

✓ exploring a range of everyday liquids and observing how objects fall through them

✓ planning a fair test to compare the rate of movement of a marble through liquids

✓ designing and making a timer

✓ taking part in an Odd one out activity

✓ systematically Classifying and grouping their results

✓ creating a marble dropping device

✓ using dance to communicate ideas about liquids

You should see evidence of their thinking and learning in:

✓ how they describe their observations to you and each other

✓ how they carry out their investigation

✓ their contributions to the Odd one out activity

✓ their Classifying and grouping table

✓ their tables, graphs and branching databases

✓ the things that they design and make.

✓ their suggestions for improvement to others in their group or class

✓ the content of the dance and their views about it

What children do

Discussing the Odd One Out statements

Reviewing the learning

? If you investigated marbles and liquids using a fair test enquiry again, is there anything that you would change?

? Tell me how your investigations helped you when you were trying to design your timer.

? How did teamwork help and how useful was the feedback from your classmates?

? What have you learned about liquids that you didn't know before?

SHARING MEMORY

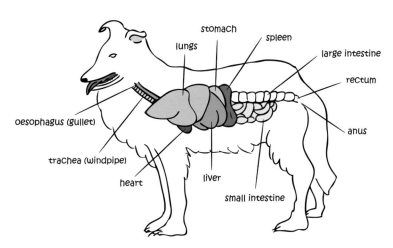

What it is

In this challenging activity, children use the Sharing Memory strategy to work together as a team to reproduce an image or diagram. The best results are achieved when the team supports each member through the process. This activity works in other subjects, e.g. geography (maps), history (family trees), art (portraits) and so on.

What children learn depends on the content of the diagram. The focus of this activity is the digestive system. Working as a group to complete the image helps to develop their skills of working together.

Resources

You need:

☐ four large, clear diagrams or photographs, such as the digestive system of an animal or the organs of a flowering plant, **at least A4 size**. Laminate these if possible. Make sure you cannot see the image through the back. Alternatively, you can use an image from a class set of reference books

☐ a large sheet of paper, a pencil and/or coloured crayons for each group.

Children may run to complete their diagram in the time allowed. This should be discouraged to avoid collisions.

How to use it

Arrange four chairs, one at each corner of the room, to act as 'easels'. Place one picture on each with its image facing away from the children. Arrange the class into teams of four. If one team has fewer members, someone can go twice. Explain the task to the whole class.

Call one person from each group to view the picture nearest to them. After one minute they return to their group and attempt to draw as much of the picture as they can remember. After a minute or so, call the second member of each team to view the picture. They then return and add to the diagram started by the first team member.

Allow a little time between observations for the teams to identify parts of the diagram that need clarifying. For example, "*There's something big in this area, but what shape is it?*" This helps the next viewer to focus their attention on key information. Encourage the teams to think of strategies that help them to create accurate reproductions. Continue for a set number of turns.

Allow the groups to view each other's work, and discuss the good features of the finished diagrams and how they might be improved.

Key questions

How accurate is your drawing? How can you improve it?

What helped you to do it well?

What more do you need to find out so that you understand how the digestive system works?

How can you find out?

Extending the activity

STRATEGY:

Thinking Quilt

There is more information about this strategy in the Strategies chapter at the beginning of the book.

Give the children a Thinking Quilt worksheet. Explain to them how to work together to create sentences by linking words on the Thinking Quilt, either horizontally, vertically or diagonally. It's best to give them a set amount of time. Give them a chance to share their sentences and decide if they agree with what other groups have done. You can decide to use a different set of words. There are two versions of the worksheet **on the CD**. Digestion Thinking Quilt 2 is more demanding than Digestion Thinking Quilt 1.

Digestion - Thinking Quilt 1

Here are some words to help you create sentences about eating and digestion. Try to use as many words as you can each time. You can only use words that are next to each other – horizontally, vertically or diagonally.

sweet	teeth	tongue
starches	saliva	chew
energy	food	molars
movement	stomach	swallo...
intestines	waste food	toile...

Here is a sentence that another group wrote to start you off. What do you think ab... sentence if you want to:

Teeth use starches and saliva to che...

When you have finished, share your sentences with another group. Do you agree w... you are not sure about? How will you find answers to your questions?

Do you think the sentences would be the same if they were written about anothe...

Look, Think, Talk
© Gaynor Weavers 2012

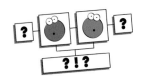

Extending the activity cont.

Compare and Contrast Graphic Organiser

Children use a Compare and Contrast Graphic Organiser to compare the digestive system of one animal with another. This generates discussion about whether all animals digest their food in the same way and about the food that animals eat. There is an activity sheet **on the CD**.

Making a List

Children create a list of the parts of the human digestive system from start to finish. Encourage them to create as long a list as possible and make a note of how each part helps to digest the food. You could start them off with a partially completed list.

For example:

      1. Teeth - Chew food   2. Saliva . . .   3. Tongue . . .

Compare lists with another group at the end. Does everyone agree?

DESIGN & TECH
ICT
Design & Technology and ICT

If the children have been learning how some animals' digestive systems can change grass into milk, they could research the products of milk such as making yogurt. Home-made and industrial processes can be compared.

Challenge children to make yogurt with a new flavour that will be attractive to other children and that is safe to eat. A survey of current favourite flavours could be undertaken. (If you do not have time to make yogurt, adding flavour to plain yogurt is another option.)

They could also investigate yogurt packaging and design a label, using an IT package, for their yogurt pots. Finally they evaluate the product and its packaging — see the final page of this section.

DANCE
DRAMA
Dance and Drama

Children imagine that they are a very small piece of food and create a dance or drama about their journey through the digestive system. They can choose the digestive systems of different animals, e.g. bird, fish, etc.

Looking for evidence of thinking and learning

In this activity children have the opportunity to:

✓ extend their knowledge of the digestive system

✓ use and explore the meaning of scientific vocabulary such as saliva, digestion, stomach, intestines, liver, gall bladder, appendix, etc.

✓ develop their ability to use research

✓ refine their skills of describing and explaining similarities and differences between animals

✓ understand how to make and evaluate a product

✓ develop their skills of working collaboratively

✓ review the work of other children and give constructive feedback

They can do this by:

✓ working as a team to recall a detailed diagram of a digestive system

✓ using correct scientific vocabulary to label the diagram

✓ creating sentences about digestion using a Thinking quilt

✓ Comparing and contrasting the digestive systems of humans and other animals and Making a list of parts of the digestive system

✓ making and packaging yogurt and evaluating the process

✓ using dance or drama to communicate ideas about digestive systems

You should see evidence of their thinking and learning in:

✓ how they describe their observations to you and each other

✓ their individual ideas about the detail in their group diagram

✓ the sentences from the Thinking quilts

✓ the content of the dance or drama and their views about it

✓ their reflection on ideas that they express in their Compare and contrast graphic organisers and/or Lists

✓ the way in which they are able to offer suggestions for improvement

✓ the way that they work as a team member and independent learner

✓ the ideas that they express when they reflect on their own learning

What children do

Reflecting on a completed drawing

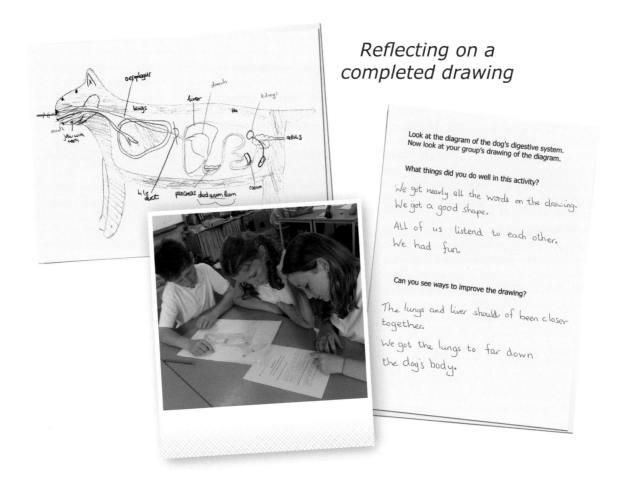

Look at the diagram of the dog's digestive system.
Now look at your group's drawing of the diagram.

What things did you do well in this activity?

We got nearly all the words on the drawing.
We got a good shape.

All of us listend to each other.
We had fun.

Can you see ways to improve the drawing?

The lungs and liver should of been closer together.

We got the lungs to far down the dog's body.

Reviewing the learning

? Is there anything that you would like to add to your group's drawing of the digestive system? If you did an activity like this again, how would you do it differently?

? Why do you think the digestive systems of humans and other animals are different?

? Did you find anything difficult about any of the activities? How did these activities help you learn about digestive systems?

? What have you learned about digestive systems that you didn't know before?

MILK EXPLOSION

What it is

Milk Explosion uses everyday liquids to show children the spectacular effect of mixing washing up liquid and a fatty substance. The unexpected reaction of the colours in the milk guarantees 'Oohhs!' and 'Wows!' from your class.

This activity helps children to learn about how different materials react together and why we use detergent for washing dishes and clothes.

Resources

For each pair or small group you need:
- ☐ 50 ml of **full fat** fresh milk
- ☐ a teaspoon of washing up liquid
- ☐ one or two food colours
- ☐ a small plastic dropper
- ☐ a cotton bud
- ☐ paper plate
- ☐ a supply of paper towels to mop up spills and drips.

 Remind children that food colour stains clothes and other absorbent materials so must be handled carefully.

How to use it

Children need the following instructions:

1. Cover the bottom of the plate with full fat milk.

2. Add one drop of each of the food colourings to the milk. Keep the drops close together.

3. Read instruction 4 carefully. Before you actually do instruction 4 discuss it with a partner and try to predict what will happen in the milk.

4. Dip the tip of the cotton bud into the washing up liquid then lightly touch it into the centre of the milk. (Be certain not to stir.) Keep it there for 10 to 15 seconds and watch what is happening.

5. Add another drop of washing up liquid to the other end of the cotton bud and try it again. Try different places in the dish.

Children can extend their observations by exploring other liquids, as well as milk, using the POEE worksheet **on the CD** as support.

Key questions

What happened when you added the washing up liquid?

What was happening in the dish once the cotton bud was removed?

What do you think is making this happen?

Why do you think washing up liquid helps to get greasy plates clean?

Extending the activity

STRATEGY:
Predict, Observe, Explore, Explain
P.O.E.E

There is more information about this strategy in the Strategies chapter at the beginning of the book.

The Liquids POEE worksheet is best used after they have carried out their investigations with milk. Give them the worksheet and explain that Kayleigh's group have been doing the same activity as they have done. Now they are trying out other liquids. Their challenge is to think about Kayleigh's group's prediction and then to complete the rest of the chart, trying things out as they go along. Afterwards they share their ideas with other groups. Do they all agree? If not why not? There is a copy of this worksheet and a blank POEE worksheet **on the CD**.

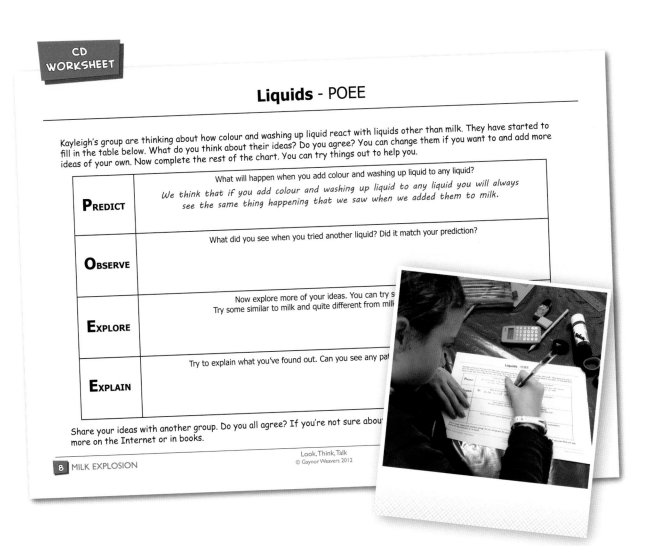

CD WORKSHEET

Liquids - POEE

Kayleigh's group are thinking about how colour and washing up liquid react with liquids other than milk. They have started to fill in the table below. What do you think about their ideas? Do you agree? You can change them if you want to and add more ideas of your own. Now complete the rest of the chart. You can try things out to help you.

PREDICT	What will happen when you add colour and washing up liquid to any liquid? *We think that if you add colour and washing up liquid to any liquid you will always see the same thing happening that we saw when we added them to milk.*
OBSERVE	What did you see when you tried another liquid? Did it match your prediction?
EXPLORE	Now explore more of your ideas. You can try s... Try some similar to milk and quite different from milk...
EXPLAIN	Try to explain what you've found out. Can you see any pat...

Share your ideas with another group. Do you all agree? If you're not sure abou...
more on the Internet or in books.

Look, Think, Talk
© Gaynor Weavers 2012

8 MILK EXPLOSION

Annotated Drawing

Ask the children to make Annotated Drawings of what is happening on their plates. This enables them to communicate more detail about their observations.

History & ICT

HISTORY

ICT

Children investigate household chores such as washing of clothes or dishes in past times compared with today. Was any sort of soap or detergent available? Can you find out how it was made?

Art, ICT and Design & Technology

ART   ICT

DESIGN & TECH

This activity links many aspects of art, such as observation, materials, colour mixing and simple printing activities. (Sadly, dipping a sheet of paper onto the milk surface does not provide useable prints as it does with a bubble painting. However, careful use of marbling inks produces a similar effect.) Using digital video and cameras to record observations brings exciting outcomes. Digital images can be used as a starting point for creative textile work.

PE

PE

Children work in groups and plan how they could recreate the swirling, dancing patterns that appear across the milk. Props such as ribbons or bands make this a more visual experience.

Looking for evidence of thinking and learning

In this activity children have the opportunity to:

- ✓ use and explore the meaning of scientific vocabulary such as detergent, fats, food colouring, react, repel, dropper, predict, observe, explore, explain, etc.
- ✓ develop effective observational skills and make predictions
- ✓ develop their ability to look for patterns
- ✓ learn more about the production of soaps and detergents currently and in the past
- ✓ learn more about how to design colourful textiles
- ✓ develop their skills of creating movement and dance patterns

They can do this by:

- ✓ making careful observations and Annotated drawings during the Milk Explosion and POEE activities
- ✓ observing and describing the effect of mixing fats and detergent such as full fat, semi-skimmed, skimmed and dried milk, milkshakes, washing up liquid, shampoo, bubble bath etc.
- ✓ investigating how soap is made today and in the past
- ✓ translating their observations into work with colour or with textiles
- ✓ devising dances from their observations of the Milk Explosion and POEE activities

You should see evidence of their thinking and learning in:

- ✓ What they say to you and group members about their observations
- ✓ what they say, write, Draw and Annotate during their observations
- ✓ their completed POEE worksheets
- ✓ the outcomes of their history investigations
- ✓ the work that they produce in their art and DT activities
- ✓ the dances that they create in their groups

What children do

Mixing food colourings with milk

Recording what happens on a POEE worksheet

Reviewing the learning

? What was the most interesting thing that you observed?

? How did the POEE activity help you learn about liquids, fats and detergents?

? Describe how you created dance movements from your observations of the Milk Explosions.

? What have you learned about fats, liquids and detergents that you didn't know before?

HABITAT BOXES

What it is

This creative cross-curricular activity encourages children to consider the components of a particular habitat. They research the living things and the physical geography of several habitats and then design and construct a scenario — a Habitat Box. This box shows a specific habitat, such as a seabed, created in a box with a lid that can be stored neatly when not in use. (See instructions **on the CD**.)

This activity helps children to learn about different habitats and the animals and plants that live there. It fits well alongside Colourful Caterpillars, Activity 2.

Resources

You need:

- ☐ empty A4 paper boxes plus their lids
- ☐ glue or other adhesives
- ☐ a variety of craft materials and tools, so that children can represent the plants, animals and land features in their habitat. Bubble wrap and sticky black dots, for example, make lovely frog spawn!

 The activity presents few foreseeable safety issues. If children are using scissors and glue the usual safety warnings are needed.

How to use it

Discuss the meaning of the term 'habitat' with the children and show them a completed Habitat Box to stimulate enthusiasm.

Give them the Habitat Box Instructions from **the CD**. Make clear any limits to the habitats that you want your class to study. Using the school environment encourages the children into hands-on research to find out what lives around the school. A broader range of habitats allows children to investigate contrasting regions.

To prevent this turning into a purely D&T or Art session, children need to concentrate on the habitat that they are 'building' and the plants and animals likely to be found there. For extra challenge and focus, ask them to include one or more food chains.

After a period of research, children produce an annotated plan of the box they would like to create. This shows the plants, animals and other features that they will include e.g. where animals live, what they eat, and any food chains that they can see. Finally, once they have completed their own Habitat Box, they can evaluate the boxes created by their classmates.

Key questions

Describe what you have chosen to include in your Habitat Box and why.

Describe any food chains shown in your Habitat Box.

How are the plants and animals adapted to their habitat?

How do their adaptations help them to survive in this habitat?

Extending the activity

STRATEGY:

Text to Table;
Table to Text

There is more information about this strategy in the Strategies chapter at the beginning of the book.

Give children the Text to Table Chart and the Fact Sheet. Their challenge is to use the Fact Sheet to finish the work that Jack and Jessica have started. They then share what they have written with other groups to see if they agree with each other. The chart can be used for other animals that the children are studying. The Chart and Fact Sheet are **on the CD**.

Habitats - Text to Table Chart

Jessica and Jack have started to complete the table below with information they have found out from their Fact Sheet about different habitats but they're not sure if they have got the right idea. Use the Fact Sheet to check their ideas and then complete the table yourself.

Habitats	Interesting facts	Large predators	Small predators	Prey	Plants
Rock pool			Shanny Prawns	Worms	Marram grass
Sand dune	Sand dunes are dry, salty, and can move about.				
Garden pond					

Now make a fact sheet about a different habitat to give to another group.

Look, Think, Talk
© Gaynor Weavers 2012

Thinking Mat

Small groups make notes on what they already know about plants and animals that live in the sea, for example. Once they have completed a Thinking Mat activity, you will have a class consensus of knowledge about specific habitats.

What's in the Box?

Put a photograph, model, drawing or suitable living example of a plant or animal in the box and challenge your class to discover what it is. The number of questions asked can be unlimited or restricted to 20, one for each child etc. Give a few clues, such as to where it lives or whether it is an animal or a plant. Greater challenge comes when the children are given no clues at all. How many questions are needed to discover what's in the box?

Art and Design & Technology

Groups evaluate the suitability of the materials used in the creation of their Habitat Boxes — fabrics, papers, glues etc. and how well the box communicates ideas about the habitat.

Drawings or paintings can be made of the Habitat Box contents from a variety of angles, including from a peep hole in the back wall. Show children famous works such as Henri Rousseau's 'Tiger in a Tropical Storm (Surprised)' and ask them to decide how to reproduce the painting in a 3D form as a Habitat Box or a large wall collage. Animals, plants and food chains evident in the paintings can be viewed, detailed and discussed.

Language

Illustrated, small information booklets about their selected habitat or ecosystem are created for a designated audience, such as a younger class.

Information relating to several animals or plants are cut into paragraphs. Children work together to try to restructure them correctly. If they are uncertain of the facts, they can research the answers from texts or the Internet.

Looking for evidence of thinking and learning

In this activity children have the opportunity to:

✓ learn more about habitats and their similarities and differences

✓ use and explore the meaning of scientific vocabulary such as habitat, ecosystem, food chain, predator, prey, desert, arctic, freshwater, saltwater, ocean, etc.

✓ learn about how plants and animals are adapted to, and survive in, different habitats

✓ develop their ability to research and communicate information

✓ develop an understanding of choosing materials for a particular purpose

✓ develop their skills of creating movement and dance patterns

They can do this by:

✓ designing and making Habitat Boxes

✓ their Habitat Boxes and the food chains that they contain

✓ evaluating the completed Habitat Boxes of their classmates

✓ working on Text to table, restructuring text activities and making information booklets

✓ taking part in Thinking mat and What's in the box? activities

✓ devising dances and games from their research of animals and plants

You should see evidence of their thinking and learning in:

✓ What they say to you and each other about habitats

✓ their completed Habitat Boxes

✓ the vocabulary they use to describe their Habitat Boxes

✓ their completed Text to table, restructured texts and information booklets

✓ the outcomes of their Thinking mats and their What's in the box? questions

✓ their reports on their own and others' Habitat Boxes

✓ the dances and games that they create in their groups

What children do

Creating Habitat Boxes

In the jungle...

...at the pond

Reviewing the learning

? What have you learned about habitats that you didn't know before?

? What surprised you about the similarities and differences between habitats?

? How did the activities help you learn about habitats?

? If you were shown some new plants and animals what features would you look at to help you decide where they might live?

MIX IT UP! 10

What it is

Mixing everyday substances captures children's attention. In these three linked mixing challenges they observe a fascinating range of phenomena. They are encouraged to think and talk about the changes they see and to offer simple explanations for what has happened.

This activity helps children to learn about how solids, liquids and gases behave, including mixing materials, dissolving, and reversible and irreversible changes. Simply describing what they see helps children to develop the concept of density beyond their normal experience of things floating and sinking in water. Some children may be able to explain what is happening in terms of density.

Resources

To do all three activities each group needs:
- ☐ 1 dropper or pipette. 5 small straight-sided transparent containers. Small plastic drinks containers, with tops cut off, are ideal because they can be disposed of at the end
- ☐ 400 ml cooking oil, 2 tsp salt, 2 tsp sand, 1 Alka Seltzer® tablet
- ☐ red food colouring, blue ice cubes dyed with food colour
- ☐ worksheet What if...? **from the CD**.

Extra substances may be needed for later follow up.

 Alka Seltzer tablets contain aspirin and their use should be supervised by an adult. If glass is used, follow the usual safety procedures. Warn children to handle food colours carefully. Clear up spills to avoid slips. N.B. Have a container available for waste oil. Do not pour it down sinks. It can be placed in a normal bin in a sealed container.

How to use it

Check your class understands each activity and highlight the important safety points, using the What if...? worksheet. Encourage children to look very closely at what is happening. Remind them to make a brief note of anything they see and write any 'What would happen if ... ?' questions on Post-its to be shared and followed up later. The outcomes of their investigations should be kept as evidence until all the ideas have been shared, then disposed of carefully. The What if...? worksheet and optional What if...? Post-its are **on the CD**.

Activity 1: Water, Oil and Ice Cube
Children fill about one third of the container with oil and then add the same amount of water. They observe what happens when a blue ice cube is added to the container and talk about what they see and why. See Appendix for additional background information.

Activity 2: Water, Oil and Salt
Children fill two containers to about one third with oil and then add the same amount of water. They colour the water red in one container and observe what happens when they add 1 teaspoon of salt to each container. They try the same thing with sand and talk about what they see and why.

Activity 3: Water, Oil and Alka Seltzer
Children fill two containers to about one third with oil and then add the same amount of water. The water is dyed red in one container. They observe what happens when they add an Alka Seltzer to each container. They talk about what they see and why.

See Appendix for additional background information. (*p156*)

Key questions

What different things did you see happening?

What ideas do you have to explain what happened?

Do you think you could change the way anything happened? How could we find out?

Do you have any more 'What would happen if ... ?' questions?

Extending the activity

STRATEGY: Concept Map

There is more information about this strategy in the Strategies chapter at the beginning of the book.

Give the children the Concept Map. Ask them to talk about the Concept Map that Lizzie and John have made and make any changes they want to. They then create sentences using the Map. Alternatively, give them a selection of cards with words such as solids, liquids, gases, dissolving, mixing, reversible/irreversible changes and density to create their own Concept Maps. Leaving some cards blank allows children to extend their ideas. There is a copy of the Concept Map **on the CD**.

CD WORKSHEET

Mixing Things - Concept Map

Lizzie and John have started to make a Concept Map but they have not finished it. They are not sure if all of the links they have made are true. Help them to finish the Concept Map. You can change what they have done if you want to.

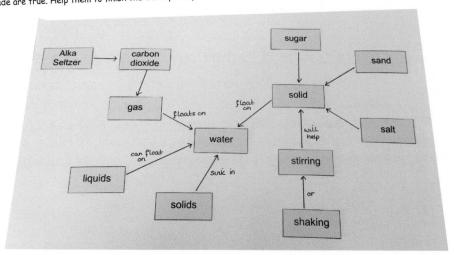

See if you can make up some sentences using your Concept Map. Share your ideas with other groups. Do you all agree?

Look, Think, Talk
© Gaynor Weavers 2012

Millgate House Education Ltd

Loop Cards

These cards encourage good listening skills and quick recall of knowledge. The activity can be played as a whole class or in groups if multiple sets of cards are available. There is a set of Loop Cards (including blank spares) **on the CD**. The cards are best used at the end of a topic on change of state and after the children have made careful observations of what happens during mixing and dissolving activities.

Create a Story

The children can create a host of unusual, colourful 'potions' from the activities above. These can be used to stimulate and illustrate stories that involve magical spells.

Link to Design & Technology, Language, Art & ICT

DESIGN & TECH

LANGUAGE

ART & ICT

The children make small, illustrated and annotated zigzag booklets of the changes that took place in the mixing activities to help develop science vocabulary and language skills. Planning, making and decorating these small booklets will use both literacy and art skills. Alternatively, the booklets could be designed and created using a computer program.

Maths

MATHS

Ideas are explored in more detail by getting the children to measure. Similarly new ideas that involve measuring quantities of liquids or solids, and timing how long things take to happen can be investigated.

Looking for evidence of thinking and learning

In this activity children have the opportunity to:

✓ extend their knowledge of melting, dissolving, and reversible and irreversible changes

✓ use and explore the meaning of scientific vocabulary such as mixture, solid, liquid, melt, dissolve, reversible, irreversible, permanent, temporary, evaporate, etc.

✓ develop their skills of comparing what happened with what they expected to happen

✓ develop their understanding of looking for patterns

✓ develop their skills of using creative ways of communicating their ideas

✓ develop their use of timing and measuring

They can do this by:

✓ observing and recording the effect of mixing various materials

✓ making predictions about outcomes before they undertake the mixing

✓ creating and modifying Concept maps

✓ engaging in the Loop card activity

✓ creating illustrated booklets and Creating stories of magical potions

✓ timing and measuring substances and changes

You should see evidence of their thinking and learning in:

✓ what they say to you and each other about their observations

✓ the predictions that they make

✓ their written, or spoken, comments after mixing the materials

✓ the links within the Concept maps

✓ their responses in the Loop card activity

✓ the content of their illustrated booklets and Stories

✓ how effectively they measure and time

What children do

*Creating a
Concept Map*

Reviewing the learning

? Which of the changes you saw were reversible and which ones were irreversible?

? What do you know about floating and sinking that helps you to explain what happened?

? If an oil tanker spills oil at sea, how do the activities help you to explain what might happen to the oil?

? What have you learned about solids, liquids and gases from these activities that you didn't know before?

WATER CYCLE SEEDLINGS

What it is

Careful observation is required for this challenging activity where children look closely at what happens when seeds are grown in two different contexts. The first tray allows water to reach seeds via a 'mini Water Cycle' and the seeds develop successfully; the second tray is completely dry and the seeds do not grow successfully. Children are challenged to think about what they have seen and talk to members of their group to try to work out explanations for what happened.

This activity helps children to learn about the Water Cycle and apply their understanding of seed germination and growth.

Resources

Each pair or small group will need:
- ☑ two small seed trays or other suitable containers, clingfilm
- ☑ fast growing seeds, such as cress, mustard or grass
- ☑ completely **dry** compost N.B. If the compost is damp, seeds will germinate in both trays (dry the compost by leaving it on newspaper in a warm place or baking it briefly in a warm oven)
- ☑ a small plastic dish no higher than the sides of the seed trays.

Follow the usual guidelines for working with seeds and plants. Avoid treated seeds. Use compost rather than soil to avoid possible contact with undesirable microorganisms. Wash hands after handling the compost.

How to use it

You can do this as a whole class activity if resources are limited but it is better done in small groups.

- Almost fill both trays with dry compost. Label the trays A and B.
- Push the small plastic dish into the compost in the middle of Tray A.
- Sprinkle seeds over the compost in both trays and finish with a final *thin* sprinkling of compost to cover the seeds.
- Add water to the dish in Tray A until it is almost full, and cover both trays with the cling film.
- Leave trays in a warm area with good daylight, and record any changes.
- Ask the children to predict what they think will happen over the next few days.

A simple 'Water Cycle' is produced in the first tray, as water condenses on the cling film and falls onto the compost. In this way, 'rain' reaches the compost and the seeds develop successfully compared with the 'unwatered' seeds in the second tray.

Key questions

Apart from the seeds growing, what else was different in the two trays?

Why do you think the seeds grew differently in each tray?

We call the way that water evaporates then falls as rain 'The Water Cycle' Why do you think it is called that?

How does what happened to the water in Tray A help you to explain where rain comes from?

Extending the activity

STRATEGY:
Whole-Parts Graphic Organiser

There is more information about this strategy in the Strategies chapter at the beginning of the book.

Give your class time to read and discuss the Whole-Parts Graphic Organiser about the Water Cycle. Tell them that they need to think about the separate parts of the cycle and how each of those parts has a different role in recycling water. There are deliberate mistakes included on the sheet to encourage them to look carefully. They need to decide whether they agree with each comment before completing the graphic organiser. There is a copy of this worksheet **on the CD**.

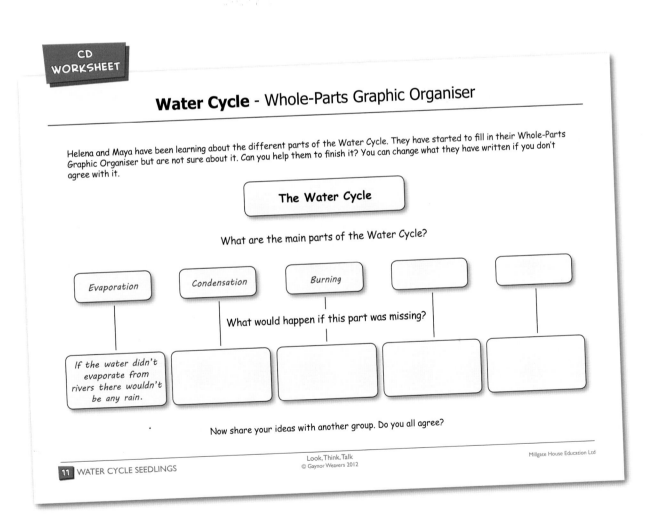

CD WORKSHEET

Water Cycle - Whole-Parts Graphic Organiser

Helena and Maya have been learning about the different parts of the Water Cycle. They have started to fill in their Whole-Parts Graphic Organiser but are not sure about it. Can you help them to finish it? You can change what they have written if you don't agree with it.

The Water Cycle

What are the main parts of the Water Cycle?

| Evaporation | Condensation | Burning | | |

What would happen if this part was missing?

| If the water didn't evaporate from rivers there wouldn't be any rain. | | | |

Now share your ideas with another group. Do you all agree?

Look, Think, Talk
© Gaynor Weavers 2012

Millgate House Education Ltd

Extending the activity cont.

Question Swap

The details for Question Swap are in the Strategies section. Ask the children to prepare a set of cards, each one containing a question and its answer on the topic of the Water Cycle . In pairs, they ask, answer and swap their cards. Then they can move on to another partner. Ask them to identify any questions where they don't agree. These can be shared with the whole class.

Sequencing

Provide the children with a set of cards showing, or naming, the stages in the Water Cycle and ask them to put them in the appropriate sequence. They can add their own annotations to the complete sequence.

Language & Art

LANGUAGE

ART

Descriptions and observational drawings of developing plants will flow naturally from this activity. A variety of resources can be used to record and annotate changes and will produce a host of materials for display.

Geography

GEOGRAPHY

Make a mini-cycle by putting a small amount of water into a plastic bag, making sure that some air is trapped inside when sealing it. Place the bag on a sunny window sill, or over a radiator. Then draw a picture of the Water Cycle on the outside of the bag to show evaporation, condensation, clouds and precipitation.

Art & Drama

ART & DRAMA

Modelling the main stages of the Water Cycle helps children to understand this largely conceptual area of the curriculum. Painting watery scenes, making costumes and props and designing creative arrows and labels to illustrate their drama help to reinforce their learning.

Looking for evidence of thinking and learning

In this activity children have the opportunity to:

- ✓ develop their knowledge and understanding of the Water Cycle
- ✓ apply their understanding of germination and seed growth
- ✓ develop their ability to observe over time
- ✓ use and explore the meaning of scientific vocabulary such as precipitation, rain, water vapour, condensation, evaporation, liquid, water storage, run-off, etc.
- ✓ develop their ability to use creative arts to enhance their understanding of scientific ideas
- ✓ develop skills of making comparisons

They can do this by:

- ✓ taking part in the seed growing activity
- ✓ exploring parts of the Water Cycle in the Whole-parts graphic organiser
- ✓ engaging in the Question swap and Sequencing activities
- ✓ raising questions and talking about them with a partner
- ✓ creating mini Water Cycles
- ✓ using art and drama to explore and communicate their ideas

You should see evidence of their thinking and learning in:

- ✓ what they say to you and each other about the Water Cycle and seed germination
- ✓ records of their observations in the seed growing activity
- ✓ the spoken and written outcomes from the Whole-parts graphic organiser activity
- ✓ the outcomes of the Question swap and Sequencing activities
- ✓ their drawings of the Water Cycle
- ✓ the ways that they communicate ideas through drama and art
- ✓ the ideas they express when they reflect on their own learning

What children do

Preparing the trays

Reviewing the learning

? How many different places do you think water comes from to form the clouds that produce rain?

? Tray A was like a greenhouse, but you didn't need to add any extra water, so why do you think plants in a greenhouse need to be watered a lot?

? What did you learn about the Water Cycle that you didn't know before?

? What did you discover about how you like to learn?

HEADS

What it is

Although children are surrounded by numerous images of animals in a variety of media, they often show huge interest and surprise at their findings when they are asked to observe an animal's physical features in detail. In this simple activity children examine, compare and contrast clear photographs of the heads of large and small animals (e.g. insects, mammals, fish, etc). Children can be asked to find examples.

This activity helps children to learn about the variety found in living things and how animals are adapted to the environments in which they live.

Resources

Each group needs:

☐ a selection of large photographs or diagrams of invertebrate and vertebrate heads. (Sunday newspaper supplements or the Internet are good sources to explore.)

☐ hand lenses.

  There should not be any health and safety issues related to this activity.

How to use it

Begin by getting children to talk about some animals that they are familiar with. This can include all 5 vertebrate groups and some of the invertebrates (e.g. molluscs and insects). Ask children to think about any similarities and differences they can think of between these animals.

Next, they find or select three different images of animal heads. Finally, they examine features such as eyes, ears, mouth parts, skin or covering such as scales, and then compare and contrast these features.

These observations can be recorded in previously prepared tables or children can construct their own tables. In addition children can try to explain why certain features such as prominent canine teeth have developed in some animals but not others.

Key questions

What features of animals' heads are different? Why do you think they are different?

What are the differences between the eyes on different animals' heads?

Do all animals appear to have teeth? How are the teeth different? How does this make a difference to how they feed?

Extending the activity

There is more information about this strategy in the Strategies chapter at the beginning of the book.

Give groups of children the Graphic Organiser and the photographs. Ask them to look at the photographs to help them to compare the ant and the antelope. They correct and complete the Graphic Organiser and then share their ideas with other groups in the class. Do they agree with each other? Then ask them to complete the Blank Graphic Organiser using different animals. The Graphic Organisers and photographs are **on the CD**.

STRATEGY:
Compare and Contrast
Graphic Organiser

CD WORKSHEET

Animals - Compare and Contrast Graphic Organiser

Look at the photographs of the ant and antelope heads. Mike's group has started to fill in the table. Do you agree with their ideas? You can change them if you want to and add more of ideas your own.

Ant - Insect	Comparison	Antelope - Mammal
It is one big bone on the outside.	What is the head made of?	The skull is under the skin, is made of bone and protects the brain.
Two	Number of antennae	One
Yes, it's is near the antennae.	Is there a nose?	Yes, at the end of the head.
	What are their mouths like?	Mouth is at the pointed end of the head with lips.

Share your ideas with another group. Do you all agree?
Can you think of reasons for the similarities and differences? Were there any that you weren't sure about?
How can you find out more? Talk about your ideas with another group. Do you all agree?
Now choose 2 different animals to compare and contrast and fill in the blank grid.

Look, Think, Talk
© Gaynor Weavers 2012

...ducation Ltd

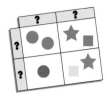

Carroll Diagrams

Children sort information into Carroll Diagrams. If focussing on the animal heads, they can easily sort for presence of a nose, antennae or ears, types of teeth, eyes, tongue, etc.

Most Likely To

Give each group of children a set of photographs of animals or habitats or foods. They answer questions such as, *'Where would you be most likely to see this animal?'*, *'Which animals are most likely to eat this food?'*, *'What makes you say that?'*

Splat!

A 3 X 3 grid of animals provides a very interesting Splat! game. Choose clues about the animal heads carefully, so that children have to concentrate on all the information that is given. **The CD** contains an A4 sheet of animal names.

History & Art

What information can children find out by studying portraits of heads? What changes can they see in modern portraits or photographs? Children can study Elizabethan and Tudor portraits and compare fashions in clothes, hair, make-up etc. Children will find animals used symbolically in some portraits. For example, those of Elizabeth I often show a pelican to denote her motherly love of her subjects, a phoenix as a symbol of the Resurrection and eternal life or dogs to represent faithfulness.

Geography

Children use world maps to investigate the wildlife of countries in different climatic zones. They can also look at the effect that climate, habitat and region have on animals' characteristics.

Looking for evidence of thinking and learning

In this activity children have the opportunity to:

✓ develop their observational skills

✓ develop their skills of comparing physical features of animals such as eyes, structures for breathing, sensing, eating, communicating, etc.

✓ develop their understanding of classifying and grouping

✓ use and explore the meaning of scientific vocabulary such as skull, antennae, mouth parts, bone, chitin, etc.

✓ learn about adaptation to the environment in animals

✓ develop their skills of sorting information onto tables and graphic organisers

They can do this by:

✓ observing a range of photographs of animal heads

✓ using Compare and contrast graphic organisers and Carroll diagrams

✓ identifying particular physical adaptations in animals

✓ responding to Most likely to questions

✓ taking part in a Splat! game

✓ analysing photographs and maps

You should see evidence of their thinking and learning in:

✓ What they say to you and each other about their observations

✓ the Compare and contrast graphic organisers and Carroll diagrams that they produce

✓ their explanations about adaptation as they view the photographs

✓ how they discuss and answer Most likely to questions

✓ how they engage in the Splat! activity

✓ their comments while analysing photographs and maps

What children do

Playing Splat!

Reviewing the learning

? How did completing the Compare and Contrast Graphic Organiser help you to learn more about animals?

? What research did you have to do to learn more about adaptation in animals?

? What have you learned about animal physical features that you didn't know before?

? What do you think are the most important features of an animal's head? Is it the same for every animal?

CAN CAN

What it is

In this simple but engaging activity children predict whether a can of fizzy cola drink and its diet equivalent will behave differently when they are put into a small tank of water.

This activity helps children to learn about floating and sinking. In addition it stimulates discussions about diet and sugar content in some commonplace soft drinks and the possible effects on dental hygiene.

Resources

You need:
- a small, transparent tank, deep enough to allow a standard can of cola to float
- a minimum of two cans of cola of the same make but ensure that one of them is the diet version
- cans/plastic bottles of other soft drinks, empty plastic bottles, sugar, sweeteners, water, salt etc. to enable them to test their ideas

Test the cans before the lesson as some drinks may vary in the way that they behave.

 If using glass tanks ensure that they can't be knocked off onto the floor. Plastic tanks are preferable. Water spills should be mopped up as soon as possible to prevent slips.

How to use it

Predict, Observe, Explore, Explain is an ideal way of introducing this activity. The children handle both cans and look for differences.

In pairs, they discuss and **predict** what might happen when both the cans are placed in the water. If your class is struggling with this, try giving them a choice of answers to vote on, such as: *Both cans will float; Both cans will sink; Only one can will float; They will float at first then sink; Etc.*

Share their ideas before they **observe** what happens when the cans are put into the water. Ask them to try to justify their thinking. The result should surprise them and sustain thinking about the problem.

Now give the children the opportunity to **explore** their ideas, for example: *Is it the drink? Is it the can? Is it the water? Is it the fizz? Is it something in the drink?* They can also extend their investigations using POEE with other drinks. Can they **explain** what happened?

See Appendix for additional background information. *(p156)*

Key questions

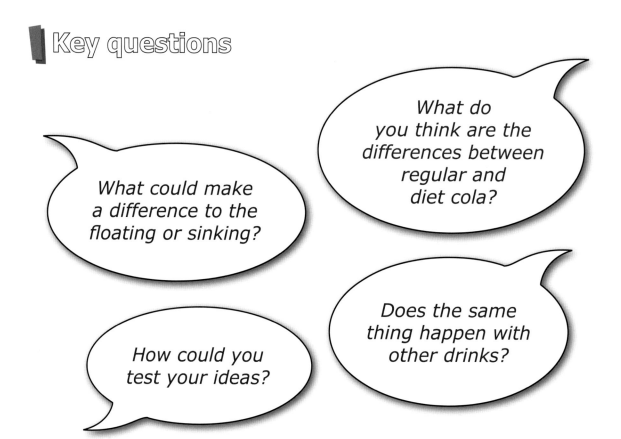

What do you think are the differences between regular and diet cola?

What could make a difference to the floating or sinking?

How could you test your ideas?

Does the same thing happen with other drinks?

Extending the activity

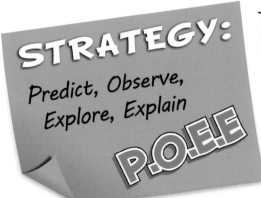

STRATEGY: Predict, Observe, Explore, Explain
P.O.E.E

There is more information about this strategy in the strategies chapter at the beginning of the book.

Give each group the POEE Table. Children discuss what they think will happen. This is followed by time to explore their different ideas to try to explain what has happened. They discuss and record their explanations. Finally they share their outcomes with other children and try to resolve any differences. There is a copy of the POEE and a Blank POEE **on the CD**.

CD WORKSHEET

Floating and Sinking - POEE

Jonti and Mo are arguing about what happens if you put canned drinks in water. They have a sheet to record what they find out. Use their sheet to help you to think about their problem.

PREDICT	Jonti says all the cans will float in the water. Do you agree?
OBSERVE	Test your prediction. What did you see?
EXPLORE	What did you try and what did you notice?
EXPLAIN	Try to explain what you found out.

Share your ideas with the other groups. Do you all agree? Do you need to try more explorations?

Look, Think, Talk
© Gaynor Weavers 2012

Millgate House Education Ltd

13 CAN CAN

Extending the activity cont.

Sentence Cards

Print on card a set of true sentences relating to floating and sinking. Cut each sentence into two and ask the children to re-form sensible sentences from the jumble.

Yes / No / Maybe So

Use the sentences from the Sentence cards game and add a few that are untrue. Read them to the class and ask for a response to each one in whatever way suits you and your children: you can use traffic light cards, a thumbs up/down/sideways system or the silent cheer/boo/shrugged shoulders method. Organise teams to add to the tension!

Posters

Pairs can produce an informative poster, aimed at dental surgeries or school dinner halls, warning of the harm that can be done to tooth enamel by sugars and phosphoric acid in cola or diet cola. Get them to review each other's posters.

MATHS | Maths

Ask the children to measure out various quantities of salt and then make up a set of salt water solutions ranging from no salt to very salty. Float a suitable object in each solution, marking and measuring its floating point each time. Children will find that salt water produces greater upthrust than fresh water and so the object will float higher.

Health and Safety: Ensure that children know not to drink salted water as it is dangerous.

LANGUAGE | Language and ICT

ICT   Ask your class to investigate the effect of cola drinks on teeth. There is lots of information on the Internet that you or they can access easily. They can also try the destructive effect of cola on eggshells.

Looking for evidence of thinking and learning

In this activity children have the opportunity to:

- ✓ extend their knowledge of floating, sinking, and the effect of sweet, acidic drinks on tooth decay
- ✓ use and explore the meaning of scientific vocabulary such as float, sink, forces, density *(for more confident learners)*, balanced, up and down, upthrust, sugar, sugar-free, etc.
- ✓ develop their ability to ask questions and plan an investigation to find the answers
- ✓ develop their skills of observing carefully, predicting an outcome and justifying their ideas
- ✓ learn how upthrust can vary in different solutions

They can do this by:

- ✓ observing the behaviour of drink cans in a tank of water
- ✓ working with the POEE worksheet
- ✓ using books and the Internet to research the contents of cola drinks and the effects of sweet, acidic drinks on teeth
- ✓ completing Sentence cards and Yes/no/maybe so activities
- ✓ mixing and testing salt solutions of increasing strength
- ✓ designing Posters about the dental harm caused by sugar and acids

You should see evidence of their thinking and learning in:

- ✓ what they say to you and each other about the cans and why they float
- ✓ the way that they engage in the activities
- ✓ their completed POEE worksheets
- ✓ their outcomes from the Sentence cards activity
- ✓ their responses in the Yes/no/maybe so activity
- ✓ their explanations of the action of sugar and phosphoric acid on tooth enamel
- ✓ the ideas that they include on their Posters

What children do

*Predicting, Observing,
Exploring, Explaining*

Reviewing the learning

? How has the Can Can activity helped improve your understanding of floating and sinking?

? What have you learned about floating and sinking that you didn't know before?

? What have you learned about commercial drinks that you think is important?

? What is the most important thing that you would tell someone about tooth decay?

BLOSSOMS

What it is

Blossoms is a fantastic 'hands on' activity where children look at the structure of flowers by dissecting them. They think and talk about what each part of the flower is for and try to identify what each part is called using card labels. Then they create a flower by choosing their own materials.

This activity helps children to learn about the different parts of flowering plants, the functions of those parts and how plants are classified. It helps them to observe and explore the fine detail of flowers and encourages their written and spoken use of plant vocabulary.

Resources

You need:
- ☑ easily available flower heads such as snowdrop, winter jasmine, tulip, wallflower, crocus, daffodil, sweet pea, poppy, star gazer lily, geranium, nasturtium or rosebay willowherb
- ☑ card strips approximately 15 cm X 8 cm, double sided tape
- ☑ small printed labels with names of flower parts (**see the CD**)
- ☑ plastic tweezers (optional)
- ☑ selection of materials to make their own flowers.

Some flowers are poisonous if eaten or can irritate the skin. If children are collecting flowers from outside, highlight any risks and the importance of hand washing after handling soil and plant materials. There is a list of hazardous plants in the A.S.E. publication, *Be safe!*

How to use it

Give each pair a flower head, labels and a strip of card. They may need to research the words to find out about each part. The Labels are **on the CD**.

Children attach double sided tape across the middle of the card. Starting at the outermost part of the base of the flower they remove all the parts that look the same with plastic tweezers or fingers. These will be the sepals. Starting on the left hand side of the card strip, the children stick the sepals a few millimetres apart. The ring of petals, the stamens and finally the carpel(s) (stigma, style and ovary) are removed and arranged to follow the sepals. Finally, the labels are added.

NB. As an extra challenge, children who are particularly dextrous can show an 'exploded view' of their flower by assembling the parts in concentric circles on a square of card just as they occur in the flower.

Each strip should now show the flower parts in the order they are found in the flower, starting from the outside. Each flower card can be covered in sticky backed plastic or laminated to preserve it. Children work in small groups to compare the different flowers. Do they all agree what each part is? Is the number of petals, sepals etc. the same? The number of parts in a flower may be used in its classification ... though there are exceptions!

Finally children create their own flower using materials of their choice.

Key questions

What parts did you find in your flower? Did they look the same as other people's flowers?

What do you notice when you count the number of petals, sepals, stamens and carpels or ovaries in different flowers?

Can you see any patterns in the number of different parts? Describe what you found out.

Extending the activity

There is more information about this strategy in the Strategies chapter at the beginning of the book.

Give each group the Living Graph showing an annual plant's growth, shown over a year, plus the Labels. Challenge the children to annotate the graph using them. Once agreement is reached, the labels can be attached to the graph. Let groups share their graphs and identify any disagreements. Give them time to see if they can find ways to resolve any differences. There is a copy of the Graph and Labels **on the CD**.

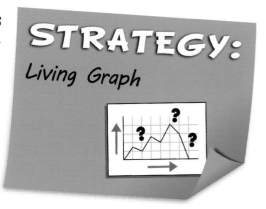

STRATEGY:
Living Graph

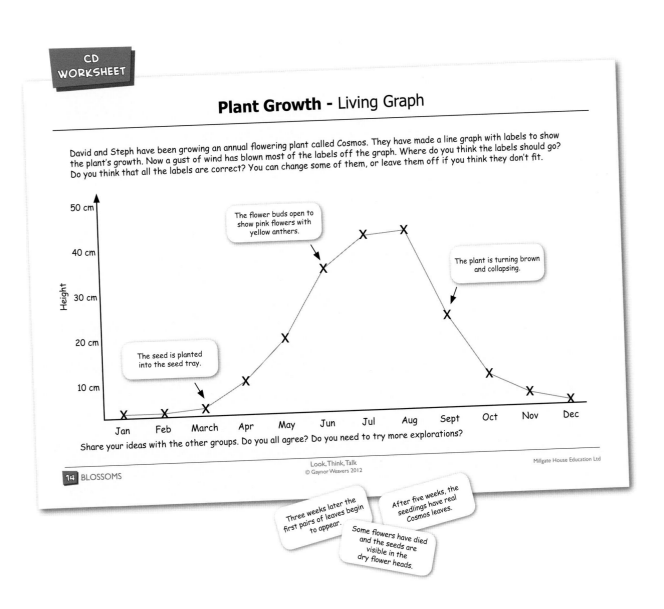

Dice Game

Children play this game in groups. Each group is given 2 dice each and a card that allocates a number to each part of a flower. They throw the dice and try to build up all the parts needed. Instructions for the game and the simple Flower Outline to be coloured in as each part is collected are included **on the CD**.

LANGUAGE

DESIGN & TECH

Language and Design & Technology

This is an opportunity for children to write instructional texts and to design and decorate an information sheet or a seed packet for an unusual or newly discovered plant. They must consider what these seeds need to grow successfully and how the seedlings should be nurtured.

MATHS

Maths

Children can create nets for the seed packets. They can also compile a database of number and arrangement of petals, sepals, flower colour, plant height, etc., look for patterns and draw bar charts of their results.

HISTORY

History

Understanding *why* scientists need a classification system to identify plants is important. There is a wealth of information available about past scientists like Linnaeus and Mendel and their studies on genetics and classification.

The Great Plant Hunt Treasure Chest from the Royal Botanic Gardens at Kew was given free to primary schools across the UK. It contains background information and creative resources to support learning about Charles Darwin and his findings.

Looking for evidence of thinking and learning

In this activity children have the opportunity to:

✓ learn about the names and functions of the parts of flowers

✓ develop their understanding of differences between flowering plants and how these differences are used to classify them

✓ use and explore the meaning of scientific vocabulary such as sepal, carpel, stamen, petal, reproduce, seeds, flowers, pollinate, etc.

✓ practice the use of instructional writing

✓ learn how to create nets, graphs and databases

✓ understand how scientific ideas develop over time

They can do this by:

✓ dissecting a flower and making flower cards

✓ looking for patterns in how each flower is constructed

✓ using a range of materials to create a flower and annotating it

✓ labelling a Living graph of plant growth

✓ taking part in the Dice game

✓ making information sheets or seed packets

✓ creating nets and compiling databases and graphs

✓ researching how classification was developed

You should see evidence of their thinking and learning in:

✓ what they say to you and each other about plant parts and their functions

✓ their annotated flower cards

✓ their artistic representations of flowers

✓ their labelled Living graphs

✓ how they take part in the Dice game

✓ the information sheets or seed packets that they produce

✓ the nets, databases and graphs that they create

✓ what they say about how plant classification was developed

What children do

Playing the Dice Game

Labelling a flowering plant

Reviewing the learning

? How did dissecting and labelling flowers and completing the Living Graph activities help you learn about the function of the parts of a flower?

? What patterns did you find in your database of flowering plant parts?

? If you were given some flowers how would you put them into groups?

? What have you learned about the function of the parts of a flower that you didn't know before?

BALLOONING

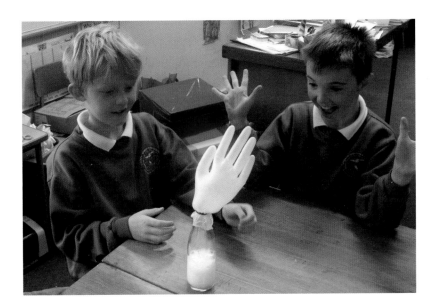

What it is

This amusing activity encourages understanding of gases and chemical change through problem-solving. It is best run as a magic trick, where a latex glove fills up with gas and appears to 'wave' at the observers. The children are unable to see that the glove is attached to a bottle in which a chemical reaction is taking place and producing quantities of carbon dioxide gas. Once they have finished giggling, they are asked to guess what has happened.

This activity helps children to learn about solids, liquids and gases and what happens when some of these are mixed.

Resources

You need:
- ▣ a transparent plastic bottle (500 ml works well)
- ▣ a thin latex glove
- ▣ a rubber band
- ▣ white vinegar and bicarbonate of soda
- ▣ a large cardboard box to conceal the bottle if you want to make the activity happen as if by magic.

Children should know what to do if substances splash their eyes. Mixing materials can be dangerous. Children should always check their plans with an adult before carrying out the activity. Check for allergies to latex.

How to use it

Put about 50 ml of white vinegar inside the bottle. Add two tablespoons of bicarbonate of soda to the inside of a latex glove. Shake it down so that it falls inside the fingers. Now attach the glove to the top of the bottle with a rubber band, making sure that none of the bicarbonate falls into the vinegar.

Find a large cardboard box, make a hole in the top and remove the back, so that you can hold the bottle securely with one hand — unseen by the children — and dangle the rubber glove out of the hole at the top.

While talking to the class, lift the glove fingers nonchalantly, allowing the bicarbonate to fall into the vinegar. Release the glove, which begins to fill with gas and move slowly on its own. (Ignore the filling glove until the children are beside themselves! Alternatively, ask the children to send thought waves to the glove to make it rise up for you.) In groups children can discuss how the 'magic' worked. Don't let them see the bottle until the discussions are complete.

Challenge your class to recreate the demonstration themselves. Give them the necessary resources in stages. First the glove, then the vinegar ... can they predict what else is needed before you reveal all? Using white vinegar can prolong the discussion, as most are more familiar with brown, malt vinegar.

Key questions

What made the glove expand and move?

What is filling the glove – solid, liquid or gas? Where did it come from?

Do you think we could create this effect with other substances?

Do you think party balloons are filled in this way?

Extending the activity

STRATEGY:

Taboo!

There is more information about this strategy in the Strategies chapter at the beginning of the book.

Each group needs a set of Taboo Cards. Children have to help their team guess the word at the top of the card without using the Taboo words below. If children are successful in their Taboo activity, challenge them to complete some blank cards to produce a Taboo game for their classmates.

There is a set of Taboo cards and some blank cards **on the CD**.

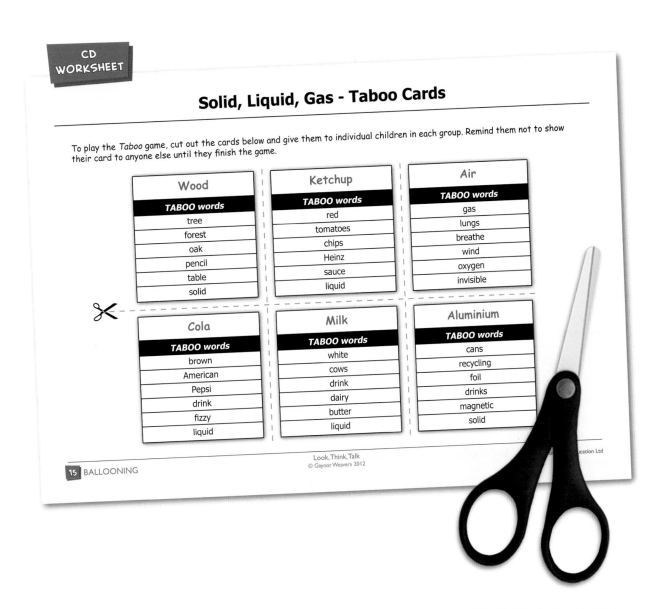

CD WORKSHEET

Solid, Liquid, Gas - Taboo Cards

To play the *Taboo* game, cut out the cards below and give them to individual children in each group. Remind them not to show their card to anyone else until they finish the game.

Wood	Ketchup	Air
TABOO words	**TABOO words**	**TABOO words**
tree	red	gas
forest	tomatoes	lungs
oak	chips	breathe
pencil	Heinz	wind
table	sauce	oxygen
solid	liquid	invisible

Cola	Milk	Aluminium
TABOO words	**TABOO words**	**TABOO words**
brown	white	cans
American	cows	recycling
Pepsi	drink	foil
drink	dairy	drinks
fizzy	butter	magnetic
liquid	liquid	solid

Look, Think, Talk
© Gaynor Weavers 2012

...ucation Ltd

Extending the activity cont.

Goldfish Bowl

Split the class into groups. Half of the groups have five minutes to discuss how the glove has filled up. They share their ideas and predictions and make sure they can answer any questions. While they do this another group watches. They reverse roles. Then they identify things where they agree and disagree. Give them some time to see if they can reach agreement.

Just a Minute

Run this game as a class activity with two teams or as a small group activity with individual opponents. Take a few minutes to review solids, liquids and gases or prepare a list for display on the board. Create a set of cards, or prepare a blank dice, with the words solid, liquid and gas. Pairs select a card or roll a dice to be allocated a state of matter. They choose an example of something that is in that state of matter and talk for one minute on the topic (e.g. They have selected liquid and talk about water for one minute). They can describe its appearance, the Water Cycle, its use, possible hazards, etc. If they say something that is incorrect, anyone can object and take over, winning a point.

LANGUAGE | Language

Allowing bicarbonate and vinegar to mix inside a sealed transparent balloon produces a reaction that can be seen, heard and felt when the balloon is held to the ear. Children can try to capture what they hear and see by writing a description or creating a poem.

MATHS | Maths

Investigate whether carbon dioxide can be weighed by using a lever balance to find out if the mass of fizzy things changes e.g. compare a bottle of bicarbonate and vinegar with and without the glove on top, compare open and closed cans of cola, Alka Seltzer in water, etc.

GEOGRAPHY | Geography and Language
LANGUAGE |

Children follow the path of a hot air balloon over a map and imagine what they will see below (e.g. rivers, mountains and other geographical features, animals, plants, human activity, etc.) and write an account of the journey.

Looking for evidence of thinking and learning

In this activity children have the opportunity to:

✓ develop their ability to use previous knowledge and understanding to make predictions, explore ideas and solve problems

✓ extend their knowledge of mixing common materials such as bicarbonate of soda and a weak acid like vinegar

✓ use and explore the meaning of scientific vocabulary such as gas, solid, liquid, carbon dioxide, acid, etc.

✓ develop ways of creating poetry from their observations

✓ learn more about maps and geographical features

They can do this by:

✓ observing and recalling mixing of materials using the correct scientific vocabulary

✓ working together with the Taboo! cards

✓ taking part in Goldfish bowl activities to help explain their observations and Just a minute strategies to rehearse their knowledge of various materials

✓ tracking a journey over an imaginary mapped landscape

You should see evidence of their thinking and learning in:

✓ how they describe their observations to you and each other

✓ the way they perform in the Goldfish bowl and Just a minute discussions

✓ the questions they ask during the Taboo! cards activity

✓ how well they work as a team member or independent learner when playing the Taboo! game

✓ the creativity and resourcefulness shown in the written accounts of the imaginary balloon journey

What children do

Playing Taboo!

Observing the 'hand'

Reviewing the learning

? How did working as a team help you to predict how and why the latex glove filled up?

? How did the activities help you to learn about solids, liquids and gases?

? Did you discover anything about how you like to learn?

? What have you learned now that you didn't know before?

SOUND CIRCUS

What it is

In the Sound Circus children look closely at what happens in five simple activities. They talk about what they have seen, felt and heard, and identify any patterns. This helps them to focus on the relationship between sound and vibrations.

The activities help children to learn about sound and the concepts of vibrations and sounds travelling in waves. This can be a challenging concept, but by making vibrations more visible children's misconceptions are highlighted and addressed.

Resources

For each group you need Guidelines from **the CD** and:
- **Act 1**: shallow dish of water, various tuning forks, paper towels
- **Act 2**: various tuning forks and a selection of ping pong and polystyrene balls fixed to lengths of cotton, paper towels
- **Act 3**: a selection of metal spoons, forks and ladles and similar items made out of plastic and wood, tied to 1 m lengths of string
- **Act 4**: metal and plastic coat hangers with a 75 cm length of string tied to each of the two lower corners
- **Act 5**: a battery powered radio or speaker, an inflated balloon and spare balloons.

In Activity 3 change the string or snip the end off before it is used by the next child. Check that the wire coat hangers do not have sharp ends. Warn children of the dangers of vibrating tuning fork prongs. Some tuning forks cause the water to make a considerable splash! Keep paper towels nearby to mop up spills and avoid slips.

How to use it

Give the Guidelines (**from the CD**) to each group and talk them through each activity highlighting the important safety points. Demonstrate how to use a tuning fork. Children will see what is happening in other groups, but it is important that they experience the activities for themselves. Remind them to look for patterns in their findings.

Activity 1 and 2: tuning fork and dish of water/ping pong balls
Tell children to explore bringing the tuning fork slowly towards the water or ping pong balls. This ensures that they see the effect of the sound waves before the tip of the fork's prongs touch the water or balls.

Activities 3 and 4: spoons or coat hangers and string
Children wind the string around the end of their index fingers and put them in their ears. They dangle, and gently hit, the different objects on the end of the string. What they hear differs according to the materials. Holding the string, spoon or coat hanger 'dampens' the effect.

Activity 5: balloon and radio
Children listen to the radio through the balloon. They can change the volume, distances and how much the balloon is inflated.

Key questions

Why do you think you hear sound differently when you use different materials?

Where did you experience vibrations in each of the activities?

Why did the ping pong ball and the water vibrate even when they weren't touched by the tuning fork?

What does this tell you about sound waves?

Extending the activity

STRATEGY:

Venn Diagram

There is more information about this strategy in the Strategies chapter at the beginning of the book.

Give the children the Venn Diagram and let them talk about what Akilah and John have done. Now ask them to talk about the five investigations and to think about how they physically experienced the sound vibrations and record their ideas on the Blank Venn Diagram. Remind them that they can put things in where the loops overlap. Were they surprised that in some cases they could see or feel rather than hear the vibrations? Can they explain this? There is a Venn Diagram and a Blank Venn Diagram **on the CD.**

CD WORKSHEET

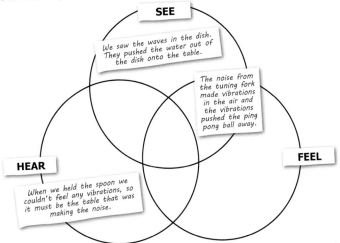

Sound - Venn Diagram

Akilah and John have done the same sound circus activities as you. They have started to fill in the Venn Diagram below to show what they learned about sound vibrations. They have sorted their ideas into what they could hear, feel and see. They are not sure if their ideas are correct. Can you add your ideas to help them complete the Venn Diagram?

SEE

We saw the waves in the dish. They pushed the water out of the dish onto the table.

The noise from the tuning fork made vibrations in the air and the vibrations pushed the ping pong ball away.

HEAR

When we held the spoon we couldn't feel any vibrations, so it must be the table that was making the noise.

FEEL

Try the activities again if you are not sure about your ideas. Now think of other things that make sounds that you can add to the Venn Diagram. For example, SEE: We saw the rice on the drum jump up and down.

Look, Think, Talk
© Gaynor Weavers 2012

Millgate House Education Ltd

16 SOUND CIRCUS

50:50

Half the class are provided with some information on sound and vibrations and the other half of the class with the remaining information. Children meet in pairs, trios or even fours. The task is to pool the information and, after discussion, produce an informative poster showing the main learning points for younger children to use next year.

What Do We Know?

Children are asked to remember one thing about sound and vibrations and write it down. They fold the paper and pass it to the next group member. This is passed on and the set of facts grow in size. Once all children have been involved, they open their sheet and share their results comparing and contrasting their ideas about sound and vibrations.

Concept Cartoon®

The Drums Concept Cartoon fits very well with this activity. Using The Drums Concept Cartoon **on the CD**, children can investigate sound.

MUSIC | Music

Children can research and explore how changing the way materials are used can alter the pitch of commercially made instruments. This can lead to children making instruments themselves.

DESIGN & TECH | Design & Technology

Research into why certain occupations require ear protection leads into a design project on making ear protectors. Children explore which materials most effectively provide insulation from sound waves.

MATHS | Maths

Children plan and carry out an investigation to find out how far away they can hear particular sounds. The outcomes can be measured, recorded and graphed.

Looking for evidence of thinking and learning

In this activity children have the opportunity to:

- ✓ develop their understanding of sound and sound vibrations
- ✓ use and explore the meaning of scientific vocabulary such as sound, vibrations, waves, reflect, dampen, travel, insulation, etc.
- ✓ learn that sounds can be dampened and how sounds can be changed
- ✓ learn the importance of insulation and how it works
- ✓ develop their ability to group information
- ✓ develop their skills of presenting their findings mathematically

They can do this by:

- ✓ taking part in the sound circus to experience visible and tangible evidence of sound waves
- ✓ completing the Venn diagram activity
- ✓ sharing ideas through the 50:50, What do we know? and Concept Cartoon activities
- ✓ using the Internet and books to research musical instruments
- ✓ making their own musical instrument
- ✓ making ear protectors
- ✓ producing tables and graphs

You should see evidence of their thinking and learning in:

- ✓ what they say to you and each other about sound and vibrations
- ✓ their records of their observations in the sound circus
- ✓ their completed Venn diagrams
- ✓ the outcomes from the 50:50, What do we know? and Concept Cartoon activities
- ✓ their explanations about how musical instruments work
- ✓ what they say or write about musical instruments they have made
- ✓ the way they make and describe their ear protectors
- ✓ the outcomes of mathematical and data handling activities such as tables and graphs

What children do

Discussing ideas for the Venn Diagram

Reviewing the learning

? How have the sound circus and Venn Diagram activities helped you develop your understanding of sound?

? Why do you think vibrations are important in helping us to hear sounds?

? How do you think ear protectors protect your ears? What does it have to do with sound waves?

? What have you learned about sound that you didn't know before?

SHAKY CHANGES

What it is

This hugely enjoyable activity astounds children. Within a matter of minutes they can make a lump of butter or a speedy salad dressing! Children compare the butter making process with that of making a salad dressing. The first activity splits the cream into solid and liquid, while the second activity combines oil and vinegar into a temporary emulsion.

This activity helps children to learn about the effect of shaking on changing materials and whether the changes are reversible or irreversible.

Resources

Each pair needs:

☐ 100 ml of **fresh**, double cream, 75 ml oil and 25 ml vinegar

☐ two small, clean, glass or plastic jars (about jampot size) with tightly fitting lids, one for the cream and one for the salad dressing

☐ stopwatch, clean cloths, greaseproof paper

☐ one of the Instruction Sheets and Record Sheets **from the CD.**

 The ingredients can make hands and containers slippery, take care if using glass jars. Follow the school's policy for food preparation.

How to use it

This activity can be done in pairs or as a small group activity, where each person shakes one of the jars for a minute. Ask the children to stop every few minutes and use their senses to detect changes to the liquids in the jars.

There is an Instruction Sheet for making butter and salad dressing **on the CD**. Children use one of the Record Sheets from **the CD** to record their initial observations.

Making butter
Butter is made by shaking the double cream in a screw top jar. The buttermilk is thrown away (unless you want to use it for baking) and the butter washed.

Making salad dressing
The salad dressing is made by shaking the oil and vinegar together. Children can investigate whether the proportions make a difference.

Unlike the cream that separates into buttermilk and butter, the two ingredients mix to form an emulsion that has the appearance of a creamy sauce. When left the ingredients separate.

Key questions

Did everyone's butter appear at the same time? Why is this?

Which part of the cream is turning into butter?

How do the ingredients look at the start and at the end?

What are the differences between the butter and the salad dressing?

Extending the activity

STRATEGY:
Compare and Contrast Graphic Organiser

There is more information about this strategy in the Strategies chapter at the beginning of the book.

Give the children time to discuss with partners what they think about the ideas that have been included on the Compare and Contrast Graphic Organiser, using their own records of shaking the cream and the oil and vinegar. They need to have completed a Record Sheet or other recording sheet of your choice. N.B. The amount of time to make butter varies so changes will occur at different times for different groups. There is a copy of the Compare and Contrast Graphic Organiser **on the CD**.

CD WORKSHEET

Butter and Salad Dressing - Compare and Contrast

Tom's group have been shaking a jar of cream and a jar of oil and vinegar. They observed the changes in the jars every minute and made a record of what they found in the table below. Unfortunately, they weren't concentrating and now they can't remember everything that happened. Do you think that their findings are correct? Can you help them to fill in the gaps? You can use your records to help you.

Cream	Time Shaken	Oil and Vinegar
Thick and white	0 minutes	Two layers
Thick and white	1 minute	
Thick and white	2 minutes	Goes lumpy
	3 minutes	
	4 minutes	
Yellow	5 minutes	
	After we stopped shaking	

Were there any that you weren't sure about? Talk to another group to compare

Look, Think, Talk
© Gaynor Weavers 2012

Odd One Out

The CD contains an Odd One Out worksheet for the children to complete that supports this strategy. Give children lists of four foods. Which is the odd one out? Is there more than one option? Ask children to explain their ideas.

DESIGN & TECH   ICT   Design & Technology and ICT

Provide the children with a class brief for making a bread product. For example, they could design a sandwich using bread provided and the butter that they have made. If they are given a budget, they could cost any filling ingredients on supermarket websites.

LANGUAGE   MATHS   Language & Maths

Children receive an email from the new local branch of Fine Fresh Foods where the Queen is coming this very afternoon to officially open the store. The delivery van has broken down and so they have no butter for the cucumber sandwiches! The Email containing this problem-solving activity and details of quantities and costs to consider is **on the CD**.

HISTORY   History

Local people can provide useful oral history. Photographs of farms and dairies allow children to observe how butter was produced in previous years.

Using role-play or freeze framing, children can recreate a story around a picture. Providing two photographs of the same place from different periods will show change over time. Libraries provide useful information about the local area. A letter to parents or a call to museum education services may supply objects for classroom work.

Looking for evidence of thinking and learning

In this activity children have the opportunity to:

- ✓ develop their ability to describe and record changes and observe over time
- ✓ use and explore the meaning of scientific vocabulary such as solid, liquid, emulsion, reversible, irreversible, etc.
- ✓ learn what happens to some substances when they are shaken
- ✓ learn how to make comparisons between observations and data
- ✓ develop their ability to compare similarities and differences
- ✓ develop their skills of solving mathematical problems set in a real life situation
- ✓ develop their skills of recording observations using all of the senses

They can do this by:

- ✓ making butter and salad dressing
- ✓ completing the Shake it up sheet
- ✓ using a Compare & contrast graphic organiser to make comparisons
- ✓ identifying and justifying differences in the Odd one out activity
- ✓ designing and creating sandwiches
- ✓ evaluating the products produced by others in the class
- ✓ calculating and costing the production of butter as part of a problem

You should see evidence of their thinking and learning in:

- ✓ what they say to you and each other about their observations
- ✓ their completed Shake it up sheet
- ✓ how they respond to the Compare and contrast graphic organiser activity
- ✓ their responses during the Odd one out activity
- ✓ how they evaluate their classmates' sandwiches
- ✓ their calculations in the problem-solving activity
- ✓ the history-related questions that they ask local people

What children do

Making butter...

...and eating it!

Reviewing the learning

? What surprised you about the changes that happened when you were shaking the cream and the oil and vinegar?

? How did the Odd One Out activity make you think about similarities and differences between different foods?

? What have you learned that you didn't know before?

? Use what you have learnt to try to explain why oil spills at sea are a problem.

BABYSAFE BRAINSAFE

What it is

In this intriguing activity, children are encouraged to think about how a delicate structure like an egg can be protected by surrounding it with water. They vigorously shake jars containing an egg and water. Then they talk with their group about what they have observed and relate it to how the body uses fluid as a protective mechanism — for example, a baby in amniotic fluid, or the brain in cerebrospinal fluid.

This activity helps children to learn about how the body uses protective mechanisms. They can also learn about how to keep safe by wearing extra forms of protection such as a crash helmet.

Resources

Each small group needs:
- ☑ 2 large transparent containers with tightly fitting lids
- ☑ 2 eggs
- ☑ a beaker of water
- ☑ paper towels.

 Ensure eggs are clean on the outside. Take care if using glass jars.

How to use it

Tell children, in groups, to put one of the eggs into a container with a lid, being careful not to break or crack the shell. Ask them to think about what will happen to the egg if they shake the container.

Then one member of each group grasps the container firmly by both ends and shakes it vigorously. The egg breaks very quickly and groups can discuss what has happened and why.

Now ask the children to place the remaining egg carefully into the second container and almost fill it with water. Once again they predict the outcome before grasping the container at both ends and shaking it vigorously.

The result should be quite different as it is nearly impossible to break the egg once it is protected by the water. The two containers can be examined and compared and children can talk about what made a difference and why. This activity is a simple model of what happens in the womb and in the skull. There are some differences to discuss with the class, such as the ratio of liquid to solid and the type of forces that cause the damage.

Key questions

What else protects the growing baby or the brain in a human?

If the fluid around the brain protects it, how is it still possible for people to get brain injuries?

What kinds of extra protection can you use to protect your brain from injury?

How is the egg in the container different from a baby in the womb or a brain in the skull in real life?

Extending the activity

STRATEGY: True False Statements

There is more information about this strategy in the Strategies chapter at the beginning of the book.

Give the children the True False Statements. They discuss the statements and decide if each is true or false. Finally, they need to explain their thinking by using the word 'because'. Share the outcomes and identify and try to resolve any disagreements. If you would like a record of the children's thinking, they can write out the complete explanation. The Statements are **on the CD**.

CD WORKSHEET

Body Protection - True False Statements

Melvyn and Kiesha have been talking about the following statements to decide if they are true or false. What do you think? Talk to your partner about your ideas.

   a) The only protection that the brain has is the bone of the skull.

   b) The lungs are rubbery and protect the heart from knocks to the chest.

   c) The hip bones (pelvis) protect the kidneys.

   d) Fluid keeps human babies safe from bangs and bumps inside the womb.

   e) The liver is protected by the rib cage.

   f) Ears protect the brain from the cold air outside.

   g) The ribs protect the heart and lungs but sometimes they can damage them in an accident.

   h) The eyes are protected by tears.

Try to explain your answers using the word **'because'**. Here is what Melvyn and Kiesha wrote about statement 'd'.

'We think that this statement is false because it is the skin and fat on the mother's tummy that protects babies.'

Do you agree with what they have written? You can change the sentence if you want to. Now do the same thing for the other statements. Share your ideas with another pair. You can do some finding out if you don't agree on the answers.

Look, Think, Talk
© Gaynor Weavers 2012

Millgate House Education Ltd

Sharing Memory

Organise the class into small groups. Provide an annotated diagram of the human body with its protective features and ask the children to view it individually for a minute at a time. In their teams, and working one at a time, the groups reproduce the diagram they have seen including all parts with labels and annotations. For full details of how to use Sharing Memory see the Strategies section.

Stickers on Back

Provide the class with stickers bearing the names of protective parts of the human body (e.g. skull, fat round kidneys, hairs in the nose). Children have one of these stickers attached to their back and by using focused questions they find out which part of the body they have on their own sticker.

 Language

Children compose acrostic or descriptive poems that reveal what they have learned about the body with titles such as, 'Life without bones?' or 'Super skin'. Writing or word processing the poem so that it forms the shape of the title object allows for a range of creative possibilities.

LANGUAGE

DESIGN & TECH **Design & Technology and PSHE**

PSHE Using the Internet and the information from various road safety organisations children investigate cycling helmets. They then design an effective helmet resistant to bangs and bumps. Alternatively, they could design a container for an egg to carry it safely to the ground when dropped from 1 metre.

Looking for evidence of thinking and learning

In this activity children have the opportunity to:

- ✓ learn about the protective parts of the human body.
- ✓ develop their understanding of the strength of materials
- ✓ use and explore the meaning of scientific vocabulary such as amniotic fluid, skull, white blood cells, skin, fat, hair, melanin, etc.
- ✓ develop their understanding of how to compare what happened with what they expected to happen
- ✓ develop their ability to research information and create explanations
- ✓ learn how to communicate their understanding through poetry
- ✓ develop their skills of using models to create explanations

They can do this by:

- ✓ taking part in the jam jar activity and making predictions about outcomes
- ✓ discussing and explaining the True false statements
- ✓ engaging in Sharing memory and Stickers on back activities
- ✓ writing acrostic or other descriptive poems
- ✓ designing safety helmets or egg carriers

You should see evidence of their thinking and learning in:

- ✓ what they say to you and each other about the body's protective mechanisms and how they carry out their investigation
- ✓ the words they use in their discussions
- ✓ how they respond to the True false statements
- ✓ the outcomes of the Sharing memory and Stickers on back activities
- ✓ the poems that they create
- ✓ the designs for their safety helmets or egg carriers

What children do

Observing what happens to the eggs when the jars are shaken

Reviewing the learning

? What would you say to a younger child about how the water stops the egg from breaking in the container?

? What have you learned about protection in the human body that you didn't know before?

? Which parts of the body need extra protection? What can you do to protect them?

? What protective mechanisms do you think other animals use?

CELEBRATION CANDLES

What it is

This fascinating lesson starts with creating a 'carved' candle — a perfect gift for a celebration such as Mother's Day or Christmas. As warm wax runs over crushed ice it solidifies, trapping ice pieces that melt, leaving holes in the wax. A really beautiful effect, particularly if wax of different colours is used.

This activity helps children to learn about changes of state and what happens when things are heated and cooled.

Resources

You need:
- ☐ a new candle that will fit in a cut down, smooth-sided, bottomless washing-up liquid bottle. The sides need to be higher than the candle and there should be plenty of room to spare around the candle.
- ☐ Extra candle wax for melting (wax flakes, old candles or bits of candles are ideal)
- ☐ A bain marie (a bowl inside a saucepan of gently heated water)
- ☐ Access to a safe heat source
- ☐ Crushed ice – bought from a supermarket, or possibly free of charge from the fishmonger. Alternatively, use broken ice cubes which creates larger holes in the finished product.

 This activity may be best done initially as a demonstration. It can be done safely in **small groups with close adult supervision** so that they can make their own candle. Wax should only be melted in the bain marie with a very gentle heat to prevent it catching alight and producing noxious gases.

How to use it

Arrange the class, or small group, so that the children can clearly see what is happening. Remind them of the potential hazards of the heat source and melted wax.

- At each stage of the procedure get the children to talk about what is happening, and why. Encourage the use of appropriate scientific terms such as melting, solidifying, liquid, etc.

- Start by slowly melting the wax flakes or used candles over a **gentle** heat using a bain marie.

- Pour a small amount of melted wax into the base of the mould and stand the new candle in the middle. Leave until the wax is solid.

- Pack ice into the mould up to the height of the candle.

- Carefully pour the rest of the melted wax over the ice until it reaches the top of the candle.

- Put aside for about half an hour until the wax is hard.

- Whilst the children are waiting for candles to set they can share ideas and draw what they think the candle will look like.

- Run warm water over the outside of the bottle and gently push the candle out of the mould.

Key questions

What do you think happens to the ice as you add the warm wax?

What do you think the candle will look like once you take it out of the mould?

What do you think makes a difference to what the candle looks like?

What do you think happens to the wax and the wick as a candle burns? Can you find out more?

Extending the activity

STRATEGY:
Card Sort

There is more information about this strategy in the Strategies chapter at the beginning of the book.

Give each pair of children a copy of the True False Statements. They consider the set of statements and decide whether they agree or disagree with the statement, or it depends. They must be able to explain their thinking to another pair of classmates. Give pairs time to share their ideas with each other and to identify and try to resolve any disagreements. The Statements are **on the CD**. It includes a set of cards to cut out and discuss.

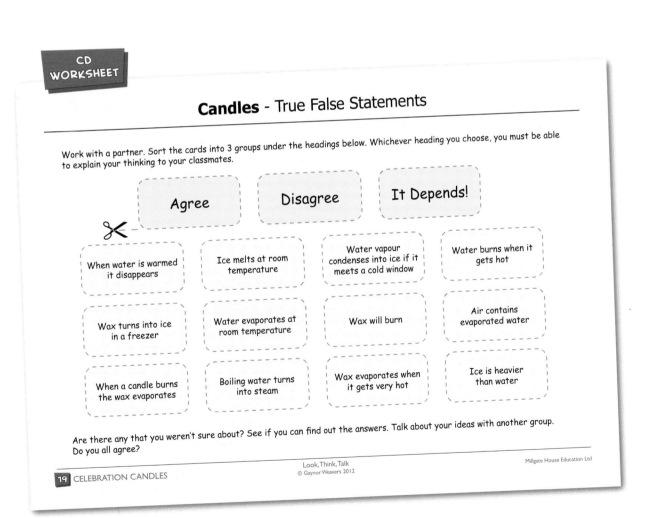

CD WORKSHEET

Candles - True False Statements

Work with a partner. Sort the cards into 3 groups under the headings below. Whichever heading you choose, you must be able to explain your thinking to your classmates.

Agree   Disagree   It Depends!

| When water is warmed it disappears | Ice melts at room temperature | Water vapour condenses into ice if it meets a cold window | Water burns when it gets hot |

| Wax turns into ice in a freezer | Water evaporates at room temperature | Wax will burn | Air contains evaporated water |

| When a candle burns the wax evaporates | Boiling water turns into steam | Wax evaporates when it gets very hot | Ice is heavier than water |

Are there any that you weren't sure about? See if you can find out the answers. Talk about your ideas with another group. Do you all agree?

Look, Think, Talk
© Gaynor Weavers 2012

Millgate House Education Ltd

19 CELEBRATION CANDLES

Concept Cartoon®

The idea of insulation fits very well with this activity. Using The Snowman's Coat Concept Cartoon **on the CD**, children can investigate ice and how to slow down or speed up its melting.

Splat!

This activity throws up an assortment of scientific words that are often confused and misused. A simple Splat! game will help children to explore and clarify definitions. Some sample vocabulary could be: freezing, melting, dissolving, separating, mixture, solution, solute, condensing, evaporating and so on.

DESIGN & TECH

MATHS

ART & ICT

Design & Technology, Maths, Art & ICT

Using nets from maths activities and a variety of suitable materials such as card, wood and textiles, children design and make gift boxes to display the candles attractively for a present. Gift tags for the gift boxes can also be created during art or ICT sessions.

RE

RE

Light is a major theme in RE. Some of the festivals where light from candles is used are Advent, Christmas, Chanukah and Divali. Activities can be linked to the topic of light and dark, or religious symbols such as infant baptism candles and the decorated Paschal or Easter candle.

HISTORY

History

Investigating how homes were provided with light in previous centuries can produce surprises for modern day children. What would life be like without electricity? Can they find out when electricity was first used in the home?

Looking for evidence of thinking and learning

In this activity children have the opportunity to:

✓ extend their knowledge of the effects of heating, cooling and insulation on different materials

✓ develop their ability to observe over time and describe changes of state

✓ use and explore the meaning of scientific vocabulary such as melt, freeze, solid, liquid, gas, evaporate, etc.

✓ understand how to make and evaluate a product

They can do this by:

✓ observing the candles being made and recording their observations

✓ taking part in a Card sort or Splat! activity

✓ producing a gift box to house their candle

✓ researching the significance of light past and present

✓ exploring the insulating properties of different materials

✓ discussing a Concept Cartoon

You should see evidence of their thinking and learning in:

✓ What they say to you and each other about their observations

✓ their records and explanations of the candle making activity

✓ the way in which they arrange cards or select words in the Card sort and Splat! activities

✓ their use of nets to produce boxes and how they evaluate the boxes

✓ their research into electricity and light from the past and its use in the present

✓ the way that they conduct their insulation enquiries

✓ the ideas they express to explain their thinking about the Concept Cartoon

What children do

Discussing the Card Sort

Reviewing the learning

? How did making the candle help you understand melting and solidifying?

? In the Card Sort activity, did any of the statements surprise you? What did you do to find out more?

? Has talking about the Concept Cartoon changed how you think about insulation? What would you say to explain it to a friend or to a younger child?

? What have you learned about melting and solidifying that you didn't know before?

COMPARATIVE CIRCUS

What it is

Familiar science investigations are connected in the Comparative Circus to highlight the importance of looking for relationships between variables. Small groups are given a limited time to explore and experiment, and to observe and record what happens. True False activities help them think and talk about links between the different factors.

This activity helps children to learn the important skills of how to make comparisons, identify relationships between variables and write conclusions based on their findings.

Resources

You need:

- ☑ True False sheets and Record sheet (optional), **on the CD** (N.B. each child needs a True False sheet if you are doing the Thinking Mat extension activity)
- ☑ ACTIVITY 1: info card, rubber bands, 5 X 100 g masses on holder, ruler
- ☑ ACTIVITY 2: info card, 3 funnels of various sizes, couscous, 2 yogurt pots, a timer
- ☑ ACTIVITY 3: info card, small ring magnets, paperclips, string
- ☑ ACTIVITY 4: info card, measuring tapes
- ☑ ACTIVITY 5: info card, 3 jam jars of various sizes, matches, 3 birthday cake candles stuck into playdough, a timer.

The use of candles needs to be supervised and hair tied back; take care when using glass; place a bucket of sand under the metal masses on the elastic bands to protect children from them falling unexpectedly: dry couscous should not be eaten.

How to use it

Take a little time to illustrate how comparative language is used at the end of an enquiry. For example, *The **longer** I stir, the **more** sugar dissolves*, or *the **harder** I bounce the ball, the **higher** it goes*, or *the **faster** I rub my hands, the **warmer** they become*.

Tell the children that their challenge is to explore links between variables in the experiment and write clear conclusions about each one. Is one thing affecting the other? Is there always a link?

Read through the Information Cards **from the CD** and highlight the key features of the apparatus.

Give each group the True False It Depends statement sheets and, if you feel it is needed, a Record Sheet. These are **on the CD**. (N.B. each child needs a True False sheet if you are doing the Thinking Mat extension activity)

As they move around the circus of activities, they record what happens and talk about the statements to decide if they fall into 'True', 'False' or 'It depends'. When they have finished, they write a conclusion for each activity using comparative language, where appropriate.

Key questions

How are the variables linked in each activity?

Was there a link between the variables in all of the activities?

Were there any conclusions that surprised you? What were they?

What difference do you think it would make if you add more masses to the rubber band?

Extending the activity

STRATEGY:
Thinking Mat

There is more information about this strategy in the Strategies chapter at the beginning of the book.

Children need their own copy of the completed True False sheets for this activity. Organise your class into new groups of 3 or 4 with their True False sheets to hand. One activity at a time, each child cuts out their True False It Depends choice and their conclusions. They then place these on the Thinking Mat **(enlarged to A3)**, in the central area where there is consensus or in their own outer box where their views differ. Their challenge is to discuss any differences and see if they can resolve them. There is a copy of the True False sheets and the Thinking Mat **on the CD**.

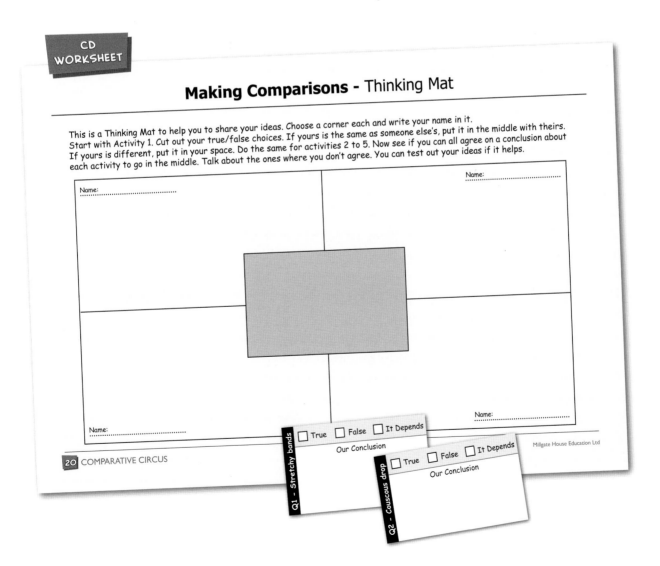

CD WORKSHEET

Making Comparisons - Thinking Mat

This is a Thinking Mat to help you to share your ideas. Choose a corner each and write your name in it. Start with Activity 1. Cut out your true/false choices. If yours is the same as someone else's, put it in the middle with theirs. If yours is different, put it in your space. Do the same for activities 2 to 5. Now see if you can all agree on a conclusion about each activity to go in the middle. Talk about the ones where you don't agree. You can test out your ideas if it helps.

Name:

Name:

Name:

Name:

Q1 - Stretchy bands
☐ True ☐ False ☐ It Depends
Our Conclusion

Q2 - Couscous drop
☐ True ☐ False ☐ It Depends
Our Conclusion

Millgate House Education Ltd

20 COMPARATIVE CIRCUS

Extending the activity cont.

Think, Pair, Share

Before the children start their investigations, ask them to consider what they think will happen, discuss these ideas with a partner and then share them with the class. This helps them to focus on the important points to observe during the activities.

KAT

Deliberate Mistakes

Ask the children to write some sentences about what they found out but to add some deliberate mistakes in the results. They swap their notes with each other and see how quickly they can spot and correct the errors. For example, small magnets are usually stronger than big magnets.

LANGUAGE **Language**

Children can use appropriate comparative words, such as shorter, longer, faster, quicker to produce simple poems.

MATHS & ICT **Maths & ICT**

Most of the activities in the circus require skills such as counting, timing, measuring and comparing. Activities can be extended to gather further data, which can be presented in tables and transformed into bar charts using IT programs.

PE **PE**

Physical exercise is a good stimulus for a range of comparative sentences. Challenge the children to find as many as they can, such as The faster I run the quicker my heart beats, The harder I throw the further the ball travels, The bigger the kick the higher the ball goes.

Looking for evidence of thinking and learning

In this activity children have the opportunity to:

✓ develop their skills of comparing the relationships between variables and looking for anomalies and patterns

✓ use and explore the meaning of scientific vocabulary such as pattern, compare, variable, data, bigger than, smaller than, etc.

✓ develop their understanding of describing and recording results and observations, and writing clear conclusions for their practical activities

✓ develop their skills of working in a group to reach a consensus

✓ develop maths skills such as measuring, counting, timing and graphing

They can do this by:

✓ taking part in the circus of activities using comparative language

✓ using the True false it depends activity

✓ completing the Thinking mat to discuss and compare results

✓ using Think, pair, share

✓ using comparative language in their poems and in PE

✓ writing and correcting sentences containing Deliberate mistakes

✓ producing tables and bar charts

You should see evidence of their thinking and learning in:

✓ what they say to you and each other about looking at data

✓ their responses to the True false it depends statements

✓ what they say after engaging in Think, pair, share

✓ how they work in the Thinking mat activity

✓ the Deliberate mistakes they write and how they correct those written by other children

✓ the comparative sentences they produce in their poems and in PE

✓ the conclusions that they write

✓ their labelled tables and bar charts

What children do

Discussing ideas for the Thinking Mat

Reviewing the learning

? How did looking closely at the results of your activities help you write your conclusions?

? How did the Thinking Mat help you discuss your ideas with your group?

? What have you learned about comparing data and writing conclusions that you didn't know before?

? Can you think of other investigations where you might use comparative language?

COLOURFUL COLUMNS

21

What it is

This fascinating activity challenges children to create a colourful column using everyday liquids. It encourages them to look carefully at how liquids behave and think about their properties, while discussing, planning and problem solving. It helps children learn about the properties of liquids and explore ideas about floating and sinking, and density.

Resources

For the Starter Activity you need:

- ▣ 3 containers of water coloured blue, red and yellow using food colouring, and 3 containers of oil coloured blue, red and yellow using powder paint, plus 6 small plastic drinks bottles

For the Main Activity each group needs:

- ▣ small pots containing about 50 ml of washing up liquid, syrup or runny honey, water, fruit juice, milk, vegetable oil, baby oil
- ▣ powder paint (to colour the oils) and food colouring
- ▣ a plastic dropping pipette in each pot
- ▣ transparent plastic tube with a stopper (see Appendix) or a small screw top drinks bottle, a saucer or dish

To add challenge, also have available other safe, everyday liquids, e.g. maple syrup, very sugary water, very salty coloured water etc.

Warn children not to drink any of the liquids. Food colour stains clothing. Do not put oil down the sink. Dispose of it in bins in sealed plastic bottles.

How to use it

Have three containers of coloured oil and three of coloured water at the front of the room. A child comes to the front and chooses one of the oils and a different colour of water. Some of each is poured into a screw top bottle and given a good shake, and left to stand. Other children do the same with different colours. As the class watches, the oil and water separate. Arrange children in small groups. Give them time to talk about what has happened and why. What they have just seen will help them with a new challenge.

The challenge:
Each group needs the Guidance Sheet **from the CD**.
The challenge is to create colour columns from the ingredients provided, plus water. They can experiment with drops of liquids on the saucers first. They need to add colours to their liquids to make their layers stand out. They should be able to produce several layers (due to the densities of the various liquids). Compare each column and give time for children to discuss with each other how they think each team has achieved its results.

N.B. Have plenty of paper towels on hand for them to wipe their dishes and mop up spills.

Key questions

Which liquids are at the top and the bottom of the column? How are they different?

Do all the oils behave in the same way? What about the syrups? Why do you think this is?

If you have two new liquids, how do you think you could work out where they will float in the column?

Extending the activity

STRATEGY:
Sequencing

There is more information about this strategy in the Strategies chapter at the beginning of the book.

Give groups a copy of the Sequencing worksheet. Ask them to look at the colour column made by David & Eleanor. The table shows the order in which the liquids floated. Do they agree that this column would 'work'? They can use their own investigations to help them. They try to predict the results of any untested liquids and finally, they can test out their predictions. There is a copy of the Sequencing worksheet **on the CD**.

Colourful Liquid Columns - Sequencing

David and Eleanor have been working with liquids to see what happens when they are mixed together.

Their table shows their results and the order that the liquids floated.

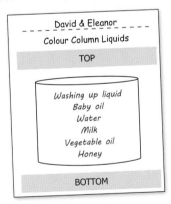

David & Eleanor
Colour Column Liquids

TOP

Washing up liquid
Baby oil
Water
Milk
Vegetable oil
Honey

BOTTOM

Think about the work that you have done with different liquids so far. Do you agree that this column would 'work'?

You can compare this table with how some liquids acted in the columns that you produced earlier. If you come across any liquids that you haven't tested, try to predict how they would behave.

Finally, you can test out all of your predictions.

Look, Think, Talk
© Gaynor Weavers 2012

Millgate House Education Ltd

Bingo! game or individual whiteboards

Provide children with a 3 X 3 grid containing the names of 9 liquids. As each description of a liquid and its properties is revealed, children cover the word with counters to get a 'full house' or scribble down the liquid's name quickly and hold up their whiteboard.

Dice Game

The aim is to produce a 'column' of 4 different liquids. Children are given a drawn outline of a tall transparent container and a numbered list of liquids. They throw 2 dice and use the total to find which liquid they can use from the list. Using what they know already, they decide whether to 'keep' it and colour it in on their sheet; if not, they have to wait till their next turn to try again. The others in the group can challenge their predictions if they suspect they are incorrect. Finally they can test out their ideas.

DESIGN & TECH | Design & Technology

A wizard needs to have 4 colourful liquids inside his magic wand for it to work properly. How will he collect these liquids, from where and in which order? What else can be added to these liquids to make them more interesting? Some liquids support the addition of sparkling glitter or small foil cut outs. Children can design and make 'magic wands' using their ideas.

LANGUAGE | Language

Ask children to produce poems about the liquids that they have experienced. Different formats can be followed: 3-word poems, 5-line poems, shape poems, Acrostic, Haiku and so on. Attempting to use correct, interesting scientific and descriptive language will stretch creativity.

DANCE & MUSIC | Dance & Music

Pairs or trios can use floor work to create a slow motion version of the liquids mixing and separating. They can compose simple musical phrases and poems to accompany their movements.

Looking for evidence of thinking and learning

In this activity children have the opportunity to:

✓ extend their knowledge of various liquids and their properties

✓ learn about how various liquids react when mixed together

✓ use and explore the meaning of scientific vocabulary such as dissolve, float, sink, mix, liquid, density, etc.

✓ develop their skills of designing and making

✓ develop their problem solving skills

✓ develop their skills of using stories, poems and dances to share their learning

✓ develop their ability to look for patterns

They can do this by:

✓ observing the colour column starter activity and making their own colour columns

✓ exploring the properties of different liquids

✓ explaining and recording what they have observed

✓ engaging in the Sequencing activity

✓ observing and predicting the outcome of explorations

✓ taking part in and explaining their ideas during the Bingo! or Dice game activity

✓ designing and making 'magic wands'

You should see evidence of their thinking and learning in:

✓ what they say to you and each other about their observations

✓ their use and understanding of liquids' properties to create columns

✓ the way in which they explain their decisions about making the colour columns

✓ the comparisons they make between each other's colour columns

✓ their responses to the Sequencing activity

✓ the outcomes of the Bingo! or Dice game activity

✓ their stories, poems and designs for 'magic wands'

What children do

Creating a Colour Column

A completed Colour Column!

Reviewing the learning

? How did making the columns of liquids help you understand about the properties of materials?

? In the dance activity, how did watching and taking part in movement help you to understand how liquids behave?

? What would you say to explain your work to a friend or to a younger child?

? What have you learned about liquids that you didn't know before?

 References

References and Bibliography

ASE Be Safe! (2011)

S Bird and L Saunders (2007) Rational Food. Sandbach: Millgate House Publishers

T Buzan (1974) Use your head. London: BBC Books.

S Naylor, B Keogh and A Goldsworthy (2004) Active Assessment: thinking, learning and assessment in science. Sandbach: Millgate House Publishers.

S Naylor and B Keogh (2010a) Concept Cartoons in Science Education (revised edition). Sandbach: Millgate House Publishers.

S Naylor and B Keogh (2010b) Science Questions CD ROM. Sandbach: Millgate House Publishers.

J Novak & B Gowin (1984) Learning how to learn. Cambridge: Cambridge University Press.

Qualifications, Curriculum & Assessment Authority for Wales (2006) The Thinking Skills and Assessment for Learning Programme,

R Schwarz, J Larisey & M A Kiser (2000) Infusion lessons: teaching critical and creative thinking in language arts. Pacific Grove: Critical thinking books & software.

M. Tibbott & G. Weavers, (1998) Curriculum Planning for Primary Schools: Science. ESIS

M. Tibbott & G. Weavers (2006) Progress in Learning: Science. ESIS & CCBC

G Weavers (2008) Made You Look, Made You Think, Made You Talk. Sandbach: Millgate House Publishers.

R White & R Gunstone (1992) Probing understanding. London, Falmer.

 Appendix

Additional Information

Activity 10: Mix It Up - For your information
1. The ice cube will fall through the oil and come to rest eventually at the interface with the water. As the ice cube melts, it will not mix with oil but the blue colouring will suffuse the water. Water is denser than oil so sinks. The density of the ice cube is between oil and liquid water but changes as the ice cube melts.
2. The salt takes some oil down, which then floats back up. If stirred salt will dissolve in the water but not the oil.
3. The Alka Seltzer tablet is denser than oil and goes straight through it. Gas from the tablet then bubbles back up.

Activity 13: Can Can - For your information
A diet version usually floats as it contains no sugar. Regular drinks may contain around 40g of sugar. This can provoke further discussion and enquiry about exactly how much sugar is in one can of the soft drink.
Cola drinks usually contain Phosphoric acid. They are more acidic than other acidic liquids such as lemon juice or vinegar. As cola drinks also contain sugar or sweeteners, we do not notice the acidity; the sweet taste masks the acid taste.

Resources (available from TTS and other suppliers)

Candle holder
Wax
Icing
Measuring cylinders
Plastic tube with stopper
Droppers
Seed trays
Sets of animal images
Transparent water tank
Plastic tweezers
Latex gloves
Plastic bottles
Tuning forks
Polystyrene balls
Magnets
Child-size disposable gloves